D1235496

GLAD RAGS

GLAD

Red Panties, Cowgirl Boots
and a Sweet Dress to Die For

RAGS

Pam Spence

EWH Press

MICHIGAN, 2014

Published by EWH Press
PO Box 537
Leslie, MI 49251
www.ewhpress.com

ISBN 978-0-9903500-1-9
EWH Press first printing, June 2014

Cover and book design by Terrie MacNicol
Cover photo by Cynthia DeGrand Photography, LLC
Edited by Jeff Stoner

Printed in the United States of America

Dedication
To my parents
David and Esther Mary Spence
who taught me to work hard
follow my dreams
and never pass up the opportunity to dance.

Table of Contents

Acknowledgements

So many people contributed their time, support, stories, photos and delightful glad rags to the writing of this book, and I am entirely grateful to all of them. To list them all would take pages and would put me in the awkward position of inadvertently leaving someone out–plus some who inspired me were strangers on the street, on Facebook or on the dance floor. Know you are loved and appreciated; know your joyful hearts inspire others and make the world a better place.

Thanks to my 'sisters of the heart' for their unwavering support and encouragement: Kate Rander, who planted the seed; Margy Day (and Steve Morse) for the space and quiet time to get it thought out and launched; Diana de la Mer for helping me over the finish line.

Thanks to my biological sister, Patricia Spence Gors, for her love, support and bemused tolerance.

Gratitude and kudos to life coach, Diana Long, who helped clear the underbrush and encouraged me to follow my heart's journey. Thanks to Doug Berch, my spiritual monkey-guru, who not only met EWH Press owners Jeff Stoner and Terrie MacNicol at a party, but who also took their business card. Even more miraculously, he was able to find it in his wallet months later and hand it to me. Working with Jeff and Terrie has been more fun than is probably legal.

Early readers who provided valuable feedback included Prof. Vicki Lefevre, Jasey and Syd Schnaars, as well as the members of the International Women's Writing Guild, Central Ohio Chapter. Excellent marketing advice and massive inspiration were provided by both Garbo Seltzer and Janna Yeshanova.

Thank you to all the wonderful people who contributed to the Kickstarter project to help get this book launched–especially Anne Tull, who worked so hard on the video and Anna Huckabee Tull who gave permission to use her great song, "I Wanna Have Some Fun" on the soundtrack. See Appendix B for a list of Kickstarter donors. Again, heartfelt thanks to each and every one of you!

Thanks to the poets who graciously gave permission to use their poems. I am humbled by your work.

Thanks to the craftspeople who created some amazing custom-made glad rags for me (I got a bit carried away while I was writing and had to indulge in some 'field research'–tee hee), including Miss G Designs and Tina's Tiaras; Zavinta Audickiene, who made my felted curlicue elf hat and Peter Jelen, who made my purple curly toed shoes.

Thanks to Prof. Arnold Ages for introducing me to the concept of the "Anger Coat" as well as to humorist Ted Roberts, who took that idea and ran with it in his "Scribbler on the Roof" column.

Gratitude to my "day-job" colleagues at the *Ohio Jewish Chronicle* and *Senior Times* newspapers who always have my back and put up with my quirkiness– Steve Pinsky, publisher and Angela Miller, advertising manager (who is still the boss of me…).

And, last but by no means least, thanks to my large, unruly family–husband, children, in-laws and grandchildren who are my heart and soul on a daily (hourly!) basis.

Several of the stories in this book were published in some form or another in other places:

Brenda Jones' "Hug Wraps" as well as Judy Good Hensley's "'da Coat" and Rae Ream's "Dream Hats" were articles written by me for Columbus, OH newspaper, *Senior Times* www.seniortimescolumbusdigital.com.

Tammy Perakis Wallace "A Red Panties Kind of Woman" was published in *TAI—The Artists' Interview*, a now-defunct on-line art e-zine where I served as fashion writer.

Portions of the piece about Marla Rose and her alpaca poncho originally appeared in her column for *The Columbus Dispatch* Columbusdispatch.com; used with permission.

Portions of the piece about Rev. Suzelle Lynch were excerpted from her article, "Suzelle Lynch's Hat Theology" in *UU World* (Sept/Oct 1995) used with permission.

Many of the other pieces (and variations thereof) were also topics on my blog: www.pamspence.com/blog

Permission to Reprint

"'What Do Women Want?'" by Kim Addonizio from *Tell Me* (Rochester: BOA Editions, 2000).

"The Love-Hat Relationship" by Aaron Belz from *Lovely, Raspberry* (Persea Books, 2010).

"Issac's Blessing" by Janet Eigner from *Cornstalk Mother* (Pudding House Publications, 2009).

"Emily Dickinson and Elvis Presley in Heaven" by Hans Ostrom from *Subjects Apprehended* (Pudding House Publications, 2000).

"The Dress" by Sarah Moskowitz (unpublished poem; permission granted by author).

Glad Rags - Photo credits

Cynthia DeGrand Photography, LLC (www.cynthiadegrand.com) cover and back photos; 35, 40, 57, 125

Michael C. Allen (www.cloudninemusical.com) xv, 137

Oshun Allen, Photographer – 4, 16, 51

Carol Greene, Photographer – 64, 111

Katie O'Neill, Photographer – 100

Author – 26, 122, 124, 135, 143, 147

Additional photos, courtesy: Judy Good Hensley (31); Joy Twesigye (140); Linda Severance Bennett (150).

Glad Rags
By Pam Spence

I've got no taste for *haute couture*
for summer's sizzling trends
Give me clothes that whistle my name
       like a crowd of rowdy friends.

A green- feathered cap I might wear to tea,
fringed chaps, perhaps, for strolling
Dance with my dollies in my peep-toed shoes
tuxedo tails for bowling.

Crackling crinolines, ruffled skirt
a flip of the hip: I'm a shameless flirt
Furtile I am, fragrant as dirt.

I'll wear them, share them
whenever I please
Memorial, Labor Day regardless
snowdrift calls for white spike shoes
boots on the beach
won't make the evening news.
Wherever I am and whatever I do…
slip on a smile and I'm marvelous.

So don't make me laugh with your codes for dress
and your power suit professional guidelines
I'm heading down the road
on my giggling toes,
anger coat trailing out behind me.

Going to wear glad rags that make me shout
unlatch that door and walk right out
 in my black lace gloves from postwar France
and my sassy-ass sassafras underpants.

Introduction

This is a book about women and clothes. Fashion, you are probably thinking: it is a book about fashion. But it is not: it is a book about courage, a book about *chutzpah*.

This is a book about the relationship of women to specific pieces of clothing that has nothing to do with fashion–although those who market fashion understand that such potential relationship exists.

As I began assembling the stories, the phrase "glad rags" popped into my head. When I googled it, I discovered that the term was first used in the late 1800s and various online dictionaries offered these slightly contradictory possibilities:

> *informal best clothes; clothes used on special occasions; showy informal or dressy clothes; informal smart clothes for a special occasion*

When all is said and done, I like the *Cambridge Dictionary Online* definition best: *someone's glad rags are their best clothes.*

I like that definition because it leaves open to personal interpretation what your 'best clothes' really are. To my mind, they are those garments, those articles of clothing, that simply make you feel good in some way: no logic, no fashion dictates, no rules and regs—just you and your piece of comfort and pizzazz. Glad rags—what this book is about.

When a woman slips into her glad rags it changes the way she feels about herself. In the interviews that follow, the woman often says, "When I put it on, I felt something shift..." or words to that effect.

How intriguing that an inanimate thing—a jacket, a pair of boots, underpants—can bring about such a profound response for someone!

And the relationship is specific to that woman: you can't capitalize on it and market the same thing to 500 other women—which is why this is not about 'fashion.' The relationship is particular to *that* woman and *that* piece of clothing. To anyone else, it is simply a dress or a hat.

To all of us who played dress up as children, we know how it works. Tie on a flowing robe and don a tinfoil crown and you are a queen. And you don't simply sit there like a lump when you are queen—you move like a queen; proclaim to all your subjects; call up the guards! Children believe in this transformation with their whole beings. You don't have to teach kids how to play dress up; it is second nature for them. They chose to be knights and queens, super heroes and priests, cowboys and astronauts. What they put on signifies who they are, regardless of what anyone else thinks.

The same thing happens to adults. When what you put on your outside reflects some important truth about you on the inside then there is something more than 'dressing' going on.

Inspiring clothes have similarly helped me maintain my sense of the wonderfulness, the slightly magical side of life, even as I have had to function in the grown-up world. I never grew tired of playing dress up. I have enjoyed clothes all my life but not in any 'fashion-conscious' way. I have enjoyed clothes for their power to reconnect me with the child who still believes that everything *is* possible; to make me more of who I want to be in the present time. My glad rags have enabled me to maintain my sanity as well as to survive in a crazy world.

For the women in the pages that follow, it was a garment or footwear or hat that they found or were given or made that they recognized as their icon, a personal marker of their hearts' desire. It was that piece of clothing that was the game changer—that struck the spark that ignited the action that transformed their lives. Their glad rags changed them in significant ways—or they changed in significant ways and wore glad rags that reflected that change—or all of the above.

I stumbled across some of these stories by accident. Some were anecdotes that I heard in passing. Others emerged as I was interviewing women in some other context—for the newspaper where I am editor, for the on-line arts journal where I was writing about eco-fashion and designers.

You will notice that throughout, I use first names only. The reason for this is two-fold: first and foremost, it is to protect the women's privacy, as some of these stories are very intimate and personal. For that same reason, in a few instances, at the request of the interviewee, I changed some names and shuffled around some identifying markers.

The other reason is that these stories are stories of Everywoman, women like you and me. The women on these pages are not famous, nor are they likely to appear on popular magazine covers or daytime talk shows. They are women you might know in your neighborhood, in your workplace or in your place of worship, women you know on a first-name basis. The women in this book are like that.

That being said, however, for those women who have a public 'face' and have created businesses or participate in a larger movement, who have a web presence or maintain an Etsy page, I have included their contact information in Appendix A should you wish to find out more. No endorsement is implied.

I loved these stories and the women who related them because they were courageous, heartbreaking, funny and inspiring—and I hope you find them as fascinating as I do. Put on your glad rags, girlfriend, and step on out.

PART I

Plucky Women, Inspiring Clothes

Pushing Back

Sophia

The first anecdote I heard was about Sophia and her glad rags. I thought at the time what a great country song it would make: it was all about a faithless man and some kickin' red cowgirl boots.

Sophia had been living with Aaron and it was a wonderful relationship—a relationship she had always dreamed of. Her two teenaged sons lived with them as well and marriage was definitely on the horizon—not a matter of 'if' but only a matter of 'when.'

And then one Sunday, after a delicious afternoon of lovemaking, when Sophia was feeling particularly content—loved and cherished—Aaron rolled over and dropped the bomb: he was in love with someone at his office. And could she move out by the end of the month.

Sophia was stunned; she was shocked. By her own account, she responded badly. She screamed and she yelled; she let the air out of the 'other woman's' tires.

But the relationship was over; there was nothing she could do that would make any difference about that one inescapable fact.

She had been a good girlfriend—a great girlfriend, she told herself. She and Aaron were made for each other—everyone said so. It wasn't fair; she was the quintessential victim. She had been done wrong; she was laid low with nowhere to go. She was really, really

angry and is often the case, when she could do nothing to change the situation, she became increasingly depressed. She felt stuck with all her bad feelings.

And then she happened to see a pair of fine red cowgirl boots at the local tractor supply store. They were standing proud and tall and she could just tell— they did not suffer fools gladly. She paid her money, took them home and pulled them on. Right then, something inside her shifted and things began to change. "They were some kick-ass boots," she says. "I knew they were just the thing to help me walk out the door from that toxic relationship."

Brenda

Brenda felt like a victim as well. A veterinary nurse, she had created a successful business, providing pet sitting for animals with health care issues. After 25 years in the business, however, a car accident resulted in a shoulder injury that put an end to her career. "I lost my business. It was three years later when we finally got to settlement—and then, one month after that, I was diagnosed with breast cancer."

Brenda says that it was the hospital gowns that finally did her in. After the dreaded diagnosis of cancer had been confirmed, she subsequently endured tests, biopsies and surgeries. But on the day she reported to the doctor's office to begin radiation therapy, the hospital gowns did it.

She was directed to a changing booth to don a hospital gown—those institutional, faded gowns we all know so well. It was ugly, barely covered her and provided no warmth or comfort whatsoever.

"It was the last straw," she said, "I totally lost it. They told me to go in there and put on a hospital gown—and you HAVE to put it on; there is no choice. I hated those hospital gowns—the fabric was thin and flimsy from being washed so many times. And it was freezing in the office. The treatment rooms are cooler, especially in the radiation room because of the machinery. When you are a cancer patient, your body is already abused because of surgery and treatment, and you feel the cold even more. The treatment can take upward of half an hour and during that time you are lying on the table with nothing on your back or chest."

Brenda pulled on two gowns in an attempt to cover herself with some degree of modesty and bundled her coat on top of that to stay warm. But she was angry.

"It was like I was a kid having a temper tantrum: I was so angry. I decided then and there to make something better. Before I even sat down again, I had this image in my head of what I wanted."

There was only one problem: Brenda did not know how to sew.

"There was like a 3 way confrontation going on in my head: there was a devil on one shoulder; an angel on the other and me in the middle. The devil would say: 'you don't even know how to sew!' and the angel would say: 'shut up! She will figure something out.'

"And I said: '*I am doing this*!'"

Harnessing the Anger

Both Sophia and Brenda encountered overwhelming pain and suffering in their lives. They were consumed with anger arising from injury that they did not choose, nor did they anticipate. And it wasn't fair: they did not 'deserve' the pain.

But, as we all know, life is not fair. You don't get to choose the cards that get dealt to you in any given game. Your choice resides in what you do with the hand you get: you can play the cards to the best of your ability, or you can fold and slink away.

Although Sophia's initial reaction was to indulge in a bit of gratuitous, but ultimately self destructive anger, the red boots, her glad rags, helped her refocus.

When she pulled on those boots, she says she felt something shift inside her. And so she marched out with her head held high: these boots were definitely

Anger Coat

I received an interesting article for consideration, written by Professor Arnold Ages of Toronto and was immediately captivated by the descriptor, 'anger coat.' Having Brenda's story freshly in my mind, I read on with fascination.

Judaic wisdom teaches that an individual is known by his 'kiso, koso and kaso,' words which may be charitably translated as generosity, sobriety and the quality of one's anger-management. Mind you, the Hebrew version, with its repetitive initial consonant, sounds much better. Moreover, in Hassidic lore the story is told of pious gentlemen who, whenever he felt a fit of anger descending upon him, would don his 'beged ka'as' or anger coat, enter a closet, close the door and sit therein until his anger passed. The story does not, of course,

made for walking. She took back that sense of self worth that she had given away—lock stock and barrel—to Aaron. She gave him her heart and handed over her own self-esteem in the bargain.

With the help of Barbara, a spiritual counselor, the two women came up with a ritual to celebrate Sophia's recovery of her sense of self. When Barbara heard the story of Sophia's red boots and the inspiration they had provided, she proposed to Sophia that they make a video of her freedom march.

Barbara and Sophia went to a nearby, entirely *upscale* mall and Barbara shot footage of Sophia and her boots. "There was an exclusive lingerie store— like Victoria Secret," says Barbara, "and the camera panned up from the boots walking into the store to Sophia's inner thigh as she tried on all manner of sexy lingerie. We then went into a very expensive jewelry store and arranged the boots in the window, alongside the diamonds and gold.

"There was a group of young Girl Scouts at the mall in their uniforms. We got them to dance around in a circle and Sophia joined in. The video focused on the boots, not on Sophia's face; it was all about those red boots and the journey."

Sophia recovered from that devastating break-up and, in the process, recovered her true self—who

tell us how many times the gentleman had to enter
his closet and how ragged his coat became.

I had never heard of this before but was inspired to dig a little deeper. In another source, I came across a description of the anger coat having "complicated fastenings." As a result, by the time the person unfastened the buttons or lacings, put on the coat, sat in the closet waiting for the anger to subside; then unfastened the coat again, hung it up and refastened the coat for the next time, the anger had ample time to dissipate, much as Brenda described her process of making many HugWraps.

When I asked a colleague if he had ever heard of the anger coat, he admitted he had not, but it quickly lodged in his imagination. He subsequently wrote a funny article having to do with a rabbi who came home for lunch, in anticipation of eating a juicy plum from his lovingly cultivated plum tree. Alas! When he arrived home, he discovered that his wife had plucked all of his prize plums to create a dessert to serve at her women's luncheon.

The rabbi flew into a rage, but wanting to observe right living and appropriately manage his anger, he stormed to the closet to find his anger coat. Unfortunately, in anticipation of her lady guests, the rabbi's wife had moved his ragged anger coat to an undisclosed location. Not only was the poor rabbi just happened to be wearing some kick-ass red boots. She went from feeling powerless to feeling entirely powerful; from depressed and stuck to energized and active. As reflected in her video, she celebrated her sexiness, her love of beautiful things, her sense of joyfulness and freedom: she was the star of her own life story.

After awhile, as she got her mojo back, Sophia handed off those boots to Cathy, a friend who was also going through a particularly painful breakup. She gave Cathy the boots and she shared her story. Sophia wished her well and then she moved on. For her part, Cathy wore the boots until they fell apart.

For Brenda, shivering in the treatment room, finding her personal power took a bit more concentrated effort as well as a healthy dose of *chutzpah.*

"I was just livid by the time I got home from the doctor's office," she recalls. "I walked in the back door of my house and the phone was ringing. I snatched it off the wall and barked 'WHAT?!' It was my girlfriend, Anne, on the other end who listened patiently as I told her about those hospital gowns and how I was going to make my own. And I said, 'The only problem is, I can't sew.'"

Brenda had made her mind up and was determined to change her circumstances—to take action, come angry, now he couldn't find his anger coat! How entirely frustrating!

Luckily, love won the day as his wife had saved the very best plum for him and served it up with his favorite tea.

On those days when everything you do turns to mud, having an anger coat hanging in the closet might not be such a bad idea!

hell or high water. As it happened, the friend on the other end of the phone, held the key she needed.

"Well, this is your lucky day," said Anne. "As it happens, I'm a pretty good seamstress and I can teach you how to sew—no problem."

With Anne's help, Brenda shopped for flannel in an array of colorful patterns, soft to the touch, and created the garments she had envisioned. She wore one to her next treatment and other patients in the waiting room sat up and took immediate notice. "Where did you get that? What is that?" they all asked her.

As she had been making the gown, it had brought to mind the image of a warm hug, says Brenda, "so I blurted out: it's a HugWrap—and I made it."

That wrap became the first of many Brenda made. "Every week was like a fashion show," she says. "The radiation department and the other patients were excited to see what I would be wearing at each appointment."

For Brenda, brought low and close to despair by the unfairness of life-threatening illness, deciding to push back and take action changed the way she felt about herself. She transformed herself from victim to active participant.

"The big thing that making the Hug Wraps did was to give me was some kind of control back over my life. The more I kept sewing, the more it brought my anger down. At the doctor's office, I wasn't just a patient number, the 9:30 appointment; I was that someone who made the HugWrap."

After the Storm, a Rainbow

In Brenda's case, she was able to extend the power of her own transformation to the care and comfort of other travelers.

When she finished her radiation therapy, Brenda washed all the HugWraps she had made and donated them to the doctor's office to give away. She told him, "If anyone is interested in using them, they were welcome to them; if not, just throw them away."

She had sewn hand made *Made by Brenda Jones* labels in the wraps and was amazed when she started getting requests for the HugWraps. "They are often ordered (or requested) for a mother or sister or daughter when people just don't know what to do. Giving the HugWrap is like giving a warm hug."

Brenda used her anger, refocused her anger, and channeled all that energy into claiming her own power. In the process, she became a role model, a heroine, to many other women as well. Anger can be a great force for change, as long as we find creative ways to use it.

Sophia and Brenda used their glad rags to step out and change themselves and in the process, they changed the world they encountered for the better as well.

Can you imagine stepping into some proud boots or wrapping yourself in a soft and colorful gown that you have made? Can you imagine how that might make you feel differently about yourself and your challenging situation? Consider what you might put on that would change the way you feel about yourself.

Indeed, there are times when we are pushed up against the wall and we come blasting back with our six-guns blazing. There are also times when we simply get pushed aside, knocked over, face down in the dust. The choice becomes clear: we can opt to stay by the wayside or we make the decision to brush ourselves off, pull up our big girl pants and take action.

2

Against All the Odds

Judy

Judy was diagnosed with Young Onset Parkinson's a few months after turning 40, a diagnosis that changed her life overnight. Parkinson's Disease (known historically as 'shaking palsy') is a degenerative neurological disease—meaning, it doesn't go away and gets worse over time. It manifests progressively in shaking of the limbs, inability to control movement, changes in gait and mobility and impaired cognitive function. There is currently no cure for the disease.

As one would expect, Judy was filled with dread. Questions flooded her mind and threatened to overwhelm her. She wondered if her family would understand and support her; if her friends would all abandon her. She wondered what would become of her.

Judy was used to being self sufficient, of taking care of business; now her head was filled with images of herself as someone who needed to be taken care of—an invalid, in the prime of life. At best, she worried about being abandoned; at the bottom of her despair, she feared a life devoid of meaning, where she would have nothing of value to contribute.

"Parkinson's disease is a very scary disease," says Judy. "I didn't know how quickly it would progress."

There were all kinds of options to consider and her mind wandered around an alien medical landscape: "I wondered about undergoing DBS—Deep Brain Stimulation, where an electrode implanted in your brain to help control tremors; I wondered if I should volunteer to be part of a clinical trial to help further research about Parkinson's.

"And, of course, I wondered if I would still be able to make a difference in this world, struggling for the rest of my life with this chronic illness."

But Judy is a survivor, a tough nut. She did not succumb to despair. After all was said and done, when the initial tidal wave of panic subsided, she got herself a new coat—and after that, everything changed.

Amy

Amy, on the other hand, was taking some shaky baby steps, trying to let go of the security of teaching school, dreaming of having her own business. Although she enjoyed the children, she felt that she would never really have control over her own life as long as she stayed in teaching.

"I loved the kids and I loved teaching—but oh, the politics in the school system!" she says. "I wanted to take off, expand; I wanted to have control over my own destiny, but at the same time, I was scared to death to try."

She began working part time as a skin care and cosmetics consultant on the side to make a little extra money, but, by her own admission, found it daunting. "I was intimidated to even hand out business cards; I did not want to intrude further by offering them a catalogue."

This shyness, she says, extended back into her childhood. "I was that girl in Girl Scouts who ate all my Girl Scout cookies because I was too shy to sell them and then had to get the money together somehow to pay for them."

She yearned to be successful and fantasized of one day earning the sales bonuses, the cars and cruises. There was a huge gulf between Amy-on-the-inside who wanted to fly and Amy-on-the-outside who didn't want to be a bother to anyone. She had a healthy, exciting fantasy life; but her self-limiting 'reality' kept her firmly chained to a pedestrian, mundane life.

She loved the products she sold and allowed herself to feel some fledgling excitement as she began to build her business. She began to think that perhaps she could make this business work after all.

And then, out of the blue, her husband left her. Overnight, she was faced with the daunting prospect of supporting herself and her three young children.

It was a terrifying situation for Amy. She had no idea of how to manage, of where to turn. And then she happened to be walking through a department store and found a pair of underpants that saved her life.

Now—you probably think I am kidding you. Perhaps you are even thinking that I am trivializing the challenges of these two women who were facing an uncertain and scary future. But in fact, the glad rags they each found became their game changer.

Judy isn't the type of person who usually wears clothes that draw attention to herself. She was a scientist and had a career as an analytical chemist. Her normal attire was 'business conservative.'

"I would usually wear slacks, blouse or a button up shirt, often a dress for church," she says. But after being diagnosed with Young Onset Parkinson's and having to go on disability, all bets were off.

On impulse, the Tennessee bred, 'old-fashioned gal' purchased a jacket on sale that she describes as 'pretty loud and colorful' and which her daughter dismissed as 'hideous.'

"I kind of just put it in the closet and when my daughter went to camp, I sent it along with her— because they do plays and things and I thought they could use it as a costume," she says.

The coat 'accidentally' got left at camp at the end of the summer with Judy's permission. "At least she asked first!" says Judy. "I didn't really mind."

But the jacket had struck a chord with Judy and so she went back to the store in search of a replacement. Luckily, the store happened to have another jacket left in that same color and pattern—and it had been reduced even further in price. Judy bought her glad rags for $7.50 cash. And she started wearing it to Parkinson's support groups and gatherings.

The jacket quickly became known as 'da Coat and has become a familiar sight at Parkinson's gatherings.

"It has served as a springboard for me to start the conversation about Parkinson's Disease," says Judy. "After giving it some thought, wearing 'da Coat kind of parallels having Parkinson's. The symptoms eventually make us stand out; we may even be ridiculed by others for standing out in such an unusual way."

Not only does Judy wear the 'da Coat to encourage and educate people, she also asks others to put the

coat on so she can photograph them. "I have over 400 photos of men, women, children and animals wearing the coat," she says. "Maybe they are just being kind, but I see it as a way of being accepting of me. If I am going to stand out, might as well make the best of it. It is my way to spread awareness of the disease and to have some fun with it."

When Judy got knocked down flat by a disease that threatened to dominate her life, she got back up, dusted herself off and transformed her sense of despair and powerless into action. Putting on that cheerful, bright orange, flowered coat ignited her courage: she was able to 'have fun' with it. It gave her newfound determination a physical manifestation, a 'face.' Attired in that marvelous coat, Judy found her voice.

"Parkinson's may be an adversity we face, but we can turn it into an advantage, a point in our favor, if we just keep a positive attitude," she says. "My Parkinson's has allowed me to meet so many wonderful people; it has helped me move out of a comfort zone into an active role in the effort to fundraise for a cure; and it has helped me become more attentive to life around me and to be more compassionate to others.

"I look around when I get down and notice other lives in darker turmoil or pain and I'm reminded that I have no reason to complain, but every reason to keep on loving, laughing, and living!"

Judy's courage is stoked by her determination: "I have taken this motto to heart: 'I *will* endure for a cure!'" she says. "And I intend to do just that and do my best to help others with this illness find hope and encouragement to face each day!"

Along the way, 'da Coat became a celebrity in its own right. "It has gone on excursions of its own," says Judy. "It has traveled to others who wanted to wear it or display it to symbolize the fight against the disease. It has spent some time in Washington State, and accompanied 'The Regulars' on their climb of Mt. Kilimanjaro." (The Regulars are a group of 'regular' people—not professional mountain climbers—led by Enzo Simone, who have committed to climb 10 mountains in 10 years to raise awareness and funds to find a cure for Alzheimer's and Parkinson's Disease.) "That was the ultimate trip for 'da Coat. I cut a little piece off the sleeve tab and they left it on top of Kilimanjaro in 2009. It has a Tennessee quarter as well as some other things related to Parkinson's Disease and The Regulars wrapped up in it."

Judy and some other 'Parkies' met up with The Regulars when they climbed Mt. Washington in New Hampshire. "I took 'da Coat with me," she says.

"It has been to the Parkinson's Unity Walk in New York City's Central Park as well as at Pier 39 in San Francisco. Wearing this wild coat has a close personal association for me. It is just like having to 'wear' the illness called Parkinson's in my life," she says.

An outrageous coat is one thing—but underwear? Finding magical underwear that gave Amy a needed shot of courage changed her life as well.

In the midst of her struggles and worries about what to do and how to pay the bills and what would become of her and the children, Amy was hurrying through a department store when a display of Super Girl underwear literally stopped her in her tracks.

She was drawn irresistibly to the colorful, cartoon inspired panties. "I said to myself, 'well, even though I'm not blonde, *I am* a Super Girl' and so I bought a pair," says Amy. "And then later, I went back and bought a *lot* of pairs."

Something changed in Amy from the bottom up, from the inside out. From that point on, whenever Amy wore her Super Girl underpants—and she wore them whenever there was a chance she would encounter a potential customer—she channeled her alter ego. "If I met someone sharp, I would think 'I am Super Girl: of course she wants my card.' And if the customer said she loved the catalogue, I would tell myself, 'of course you do; because I am Super Girl.'"

And if someone didn't want a catalogue Amy said it was a moment of great sadness for her. "I would feel so bad for them. I would think, 'if only they had they known who I am, they would have taken it.'

"When I started my little business, it had been an exciting time but then my husband left and it suddenly became very scary. I had all the same bills but only one income instead of two. I had to *be* Super Girl because there was only me in charge. If I had not succeeded, I am sure we would have lost the house."

She went from someone who was timidly waiting for customers, hoping they would like her wares, to a confident supplier who just knew they were waiting for her to show up and create magic in their lives.

Amy pulled on her Super Girl panties, stepped up to the plate and built herself a highly successful business. Not only did she earn enough to support herself and her children but she dedicated herself to helping other women launch their own businesses as well. "I never forgot that frightening feeling of being helpless and powerless," she says, "and I was determined to do whatever I could to help other women become successful so they would not have to feel like I did.

"Stepping up was a necessity and in the long run, it was a welcome challenge. Sometimes God gives you that push where you finally have to *do* something. My business has become my passion."

Perhaps you are wondering, as I did, what would happen if they stopped making Super Girl underpants? Was she relying too much on a crutch; if they disappeared, would she fall flat on her face?

"They *did* stop making them," says Amy. "But by then, I had internalized the power; it had become mine. I knew that with or without the costume, I could do it on my own."

Amy became a super star in her own Mary Kay business and, these days, is an Independent Sales Director. To date, she has earned seven cars and two diamond rings. Amazing what success a pair of Super Girl underpants set into motion!

Both Judy and Amy also drew strength from helping themselves help others which can keep you going when you would really rather just hide. When you act on your own behalf, you gain self-respect in spades. When you feel good about yourself, you discover you have lots of positive energy to share. Courage is contagious. When you stand up, you give others motivation to stand up as well, especially if you extend a helping hand in the process.

In our next chapter we consider those times when you have to stand up for yourself—and only yourself. Sometimes, it is the hardest thing you have to do.

Boss Boa

My gal pal Kerri, who manages an auto repair garage, wears her glad rags with style and sass whenever the opportunity arises. Between her fab hats and outrageous attitude, she exemplifies the glad rag experience. She posted a photo of herself on Facebook wearing one of her many feather boas, with the following comment:

> *I found out last night that if you wear a feather boa in public, people assume— and probably rightly—that if you have the moxy to wear a boa, you must be too cool to mess with. Try it... it's a blast!*

3

Making a Stand

Using glad rags as a badge of courage is readily understood when you have to go up against great odds—as was the case with Judy and Amy as well as with Sophia and Brenda.

It takes every bit as much courage, however, when your glad rags make that quiet statement of your own worth. As women, generally speaking, we are socialized to sacrifice ourselves for our children, our men, our friends in need, as well as those in our faith communities and neighborhoods.

And that is not a bad thing: I am gratified that my first impulse is to look out for others. I am not a big fan of selfishness and 'me-first.' I want to do good works and extend a helping hand, change the world for the better whenever and wherever I am able. At the same time, in the lives of many of us, there comes a moment when we need to claim our moment to say, "This is important to me," regardless of how it might seem to others.

We have to shush those voices that tell us, "Don't be so selfish! We have far more pressing things to deal with right now."

Often those voices are loudest that are in our own heads—those internal critics we know all too well. Just as often, however, the naysayers who express disapproval are our families, our loved ones—the people we value and love, the ones we hoped would understand. In many ways, it takes even more courage to be able to say to those we love, "This is for me; I am worth it. And I am going to do it regardless of what you think." Scary stuff indeed!

We might be confronted with a mountain of silence, an ocean of indifference, a bucket- load of invisibility, but we know we have to take a chance regardless. We take that risk and step out of the shadows. No fanfare, no marching band, we simply do it.

Sarah

I was interviewing Sarah for a story about a Holocaust poetry website she had launched. She happened to ask me about the book I was writing and when I told her, she shared her own memory of a dress from her youth.

Sarah was a senior in high school in 1944 and like most teenage girls, was looking forward with great excitement to her high school graduation. She dearly wanted a special dress for her special day and to be just like the other American girls with whom she shared classes.

Sarah's parents, Jewish immigrants from Eastern Europe, were sick with worry about what was happening to families left behind in the old country as Hitler was expanding his deadly programs. Communication was slow and information sparse— but even worse was the silence. What was happening? Where were the siblings, cousins, grandparents, all the neighbors and friends? Were they safe? Had they escaped? Were they prisoners? Were they all dead?

But Sarah was a teenager and she was graduating. She wanted to be like everyone else, here in America, away from the politics of the old country. They had left all that behind, hadn't they?

Her parents were dismissive. Living in a nightmare state of unknowing, they wandered numbly through those dark days. Who could think of something so trivial, so unimportant at a time like this? What was wrong with her? This was no time to be thinking about a dress, of all things.

But Sarah still wanted a dress and she was determined to make it happen, one way or another.

Kate

For Kate, it was a silk jacket that became the game-changer, her touchstone.

When Kate met Bill, it was the meeting of two dedicated, earth-loving souls. Individually and together they were committed to living simply and respectfully on the land, as well as living entirely within their means. Bill was determined to pay off his land before he began building the house and so erected a tipi in the woods where he lived.

Kate joined him and they lived together on the land for a number of years through summer and winter, wildflowers and snow.

"Living in the tipi was a sensate time," she says. "Even now when I dust a cake or bread with flour, it has that sound that reminds me of the snow drifting onto the tipi."

They both worked other jobs—Bill was a carpenter and Kate a pastry chef and wedding cake designer in the college town. "I dressed in practical clothes all the time; we were living in the tipi and beginning to build the foundation for our house. I felt very androgynous," she says.

It was a challenging life but Kate had made her choice freely. And she was no stranger to sacrifice. A decade earlier, she had been in the noviate, a first step into the convent—her sites set on becoming a Catholic nun. Now, instead of a nun's habit, but still every bit a uniform, her daily attire consisted of work boots, sturdy jeans and down jackets. There was neither money nor reason for frill or fluff.

Kate's resolve was sorely tested, however, when the February rains came. "It was raining and cold for weeks and weeks. Even the inside lining of the tipi was wet. We had carpets and plastic but everything was wet and stayed wet; even the firewood was wet. We were commuting to jobs in town and it was such a despairing time."

Kate frequented a small shop in the downtown mall filled with beautiful decorative pieces and fragrant wares. "They had essential oils—amber and heliotrope, body lotions."

The shop also carried clothing. In the middle of that miserable wet and cold February, Kate saw a silk, Chinese jacket. "I tried it on. I knew it was the most impractical garment I had ever seen. But when I put it on—it was a gorgeous green/turquoise silk and reversible—I reveled in it. It was feminine, beautiful. I loved it."

Kate knew better than to mention the jacket to Bill, as he had no patience with such frippery. There was no space in his hardcore, practical life for such non-essential indulgence. Every dollar they made was one less dollar they owed on the land. Being self-sufficient was the only goal worth sweating for.

But Kate yearned for it.

Barbara

For Barbara, divorced and in her late forties, she had no one to struggle with other than herself and her internal critic. She was facing down her entry into the rite of passage that, in her mother's generation, was not spoken of except in hushed and cryptic phrases. It was a mysterious and somewhat frightening prospect.

"My mother never spoke of her passage through menopause," says Barbara, "no one I knew spoke of it. It was a major portal I was about to pass through that was shrouded in mystery... I was entering unknown territory..."

She wanted something to signify this time, some personal icon that would give her courage for the unknown experience that she now faced. What could it possibly be?

Barbara had a childhood photograph of herself that she had always loved "My father took my favorite photograph of me the year I turned six. I'm wearing my favorite dress, my new red cowboy boots and a six-gun holster wrapped low around my hips. I am rocking on my heels, with a Cheshire Cat grin, showing the camera the space where my front teeth used to be…" she says.

"In the town where we lived at the edge of the desert, in the window of the one shoe store, one day I glimpsed a pair of small, red cowboy boots, just my size. I awoke one morning to discover them in my room, at the foot of my bed. They seemed a gift from God, since I had prayed so hard for them.

"Excitedly, I slipped into the striped dress I loved, buckled the six-guns around my waist—then slowly, with heart pounding, slid my bare feet reverently into those red boots. I felt in that moment, a quantum shift in the person I knew myself to be, as the girl in me joined herself to the legions of adventurers who sought wrongs to right. Moments later, the lens of my father's camera captured this moment."

Barbara longed for that feeling again—or at least the grown up version of it. What would trigger that feeling, that sense of destiny, of power reclaimed? She didn't know at that moment, but Barbara resolved to find out.

It Matters to Me

For these women, the glad rags they sought, yearned for, were not in the service of something else; there was no 'noble cause' in the mix. They were not up against life threatening disease or pure physical survival; they were not fuelled by the need to *accomplish* something through their glad rags. But for each of them, the need for this thing—this piece of clothing—was a manifestation of their soul journey.

And how important is that? To almost anyone else, not important at all but to these women, at that point in time, it was crucial.

Sarah's Solution

And so while Sarah's parents were out, she took down her bedroom curtains and *made* herself a dress. Her mother was angry and indignant—but

Sarah had already cut the curtains and there was no turning back.

She confesses that she was not skilled as a seamstress and prayed that the seams would hold through the ceremony. Her parents could not understand why she would do such a thing.

In her 80s, after having retired from a life of teaching at California State Northridge, Sarah has recently launched a website, *Poetry in Hell*. She has spent the last 10 years or more translating poetry that was written in the Warsaw Ghetto, hidden and buried in milk cans, the night before the Ghetto was liquidated.

Throughout her life, Sarah was very much influenced by the events that haunted her high school years. But in the midst of all of that, Sarah was determined to have a dress—a beacon of hope, a resounding 'yes' to life, against all the odds.

Kate's Decision

Kate knew she had to have that beautiful silk jacket, impractical or not. Although she could not purchase it immediately, she put money down and paid it off over time with the income from her baking.

"It was like giving myself a diamond," she says. "It was the fanciest piece of clothing I had ever owned. I had always loved beautiful fabrics. And the color was so rich—it was such a contrast to those dreary days."

Thirty some years later, she has it still. She and Bill have parted company and she came home from the wilderness. But she still has that jacket. "I have worn it through the years to friends' weddings. I have

The Dress

By Sarah Moskovitz

I am sewing a dress for my high school graduation.
I've taken down my bedroom curtains-
floral seersucker on white background.
My parents come home
They look shocked
"What are you doing?"
"I want to go to my graduation"
Too late for me to hang the curtains back -
I've cut them dress length.

It is spring 1944 and they are trapped in a fog
of worry for their families in Poland,
Warsaw and Biala Podlaska
I live in a house inhabited by spirits of people
who may be dead
and may not be dead:
my aunts, uncles and many cousins,
some my age.

Dead or alive
they come up out of dark pits in the hall;
they are in the living room crying
where the Yiddish newspapers with pictures
of concentration camp corpses are stacked.
They come up
from under the kitchen table where my parents sigh

and talk softly *Nisht kayn vort shoin azoi lang*
(Not a word, so long already...)
Their anxiety is a jagged black wall of broken glass
I cannot touch, let alone cross.

I go to the graduation myself in the dress I made
I am not really good with the sewing machine
And have basted most of the dress by hand
I pray the seams will hold.
After the ceremony I watch the others
Meet with parents, families.
In cozy animated little circles
they stand, talking, smiling, celebrating something.

White dogwoods, purple lilacs are in bloom
The scent of fresh green
around the auditorium was strong
Inside my blooming young girl's body -
a bare tree charred by fire in autumn.

I walk home slowly down Chestnut Street
into the quiet in our apartment.
Little brother having his afternoon nap.
Father sitting at his desk reading the newspaper.
Mother in the kitchen ironing.

It's a long time before she asks
Nu, how was it?
I can find no words.

not worn it a lot—but it is reversible, so I have worn the brown side with jeans and the turquoise side with summer dresses. It has been my companion on my journey."

And, she says, she will never forget how in the midst of rain and mud and dreariness, that silk jacket lifted her spirits. "I sacrificed a lot in the service of that dream—but that jacket became my touchstone, an icon of who I am—a woman who still loves the beautiful and the sensuous part of life even in the midst of hardship."

Barbara's Icon

As Barbara contemplated her next step and her necessary icon, she shared her journey with her friend, Susan, around a campfire one night.

"Our conversation sparked that memory of myself as a child, the year I lost my two front teeth. I remembered aloud the red boots and the remarkable feelings of power and potency that I felt when I put them on. No sooner had I finished telling my tale than we resolved to embark on a quest for a pair of magical boots—ones to wear while walking through the Portal of Change.

"Laughing at ourselves, we spent an entire Sunday afternoon slipping our feet into all sorts of boots, seeking the feeling that would summon the smile worn by that girl in the photo, forty years ago. The rational, 'grownup' me kept being drawn toward practical boots, particularly as I looked at the price tags. But my girlfriend kept reminding me of our quest, refusing to let me lapse into my grownup mindset. My gaze was finally drawn to a pair of buffalo skin boots adorned with red and yellow lightening bolts illumining their dark sides. I felt my heart beat faster as I slipped my feet into them. Looking in the mirror, I saw the smile I'd been seeking burst through my eyes, surprising me into laughter."

For each of these women, something powerful shifted when they found their glad rags, something deep inside them.

When Sarah translated the poems from the Warsaw Ghetto, some criticized her for including *all* of them—they argued that some of that stuff was not 'good enough' and should not have been included. But in Sarah's opinion the risks those people took in terms of writing *anything* and then caring enough to save it required that she honor their efforts.

Perhaps her own experience of making the dress—imperfect and lumpy as it might have been, and risking her parents' censure—pre-disposed her to understanding what was at stake and why honoring the effort was important.

Others may never know the why and the wherefore, but we must do the thing we are called to do. Our soul survival depends on it. When we put on our glad rags all sorts of things suddenly become possible, things we might never have considered otherwise.

Step right up! In the next chapter the show is about to begin.

Fake It 'Til You Make It

If there is one thing the glad rags experience does particularly well, it is to give you a strong helping of *chutzpah*—putting on a bit of brass and sass and trusting yourself to expand into it. You know that feeling when you put on your 'power suit' to wear on an interview, or when you slip into a particularly snarky dress to attract a tender-hearted fellow at the church supper.

You might not always *feel* like a million dollars, but if you dress like you do, pretty soon people start treating you like that image you are projecting.

Helen

Helen spent her childhood practicing dressing like the woman she wanted to become—one day. Growing up with five brothers and a sister in the public housing projects of San Francisco, her taste for the 'finer things of life' was a dream she carried in her heart. "We had what we needed, but not much more," she says.

"My father died and my mom took care of us on her waitress' salary. It was rough for us—although nothing like it is now. We lived in poverty, but we were blessed: we could still play outside. My old neighborhood is like a war zone now."

Helen was inspired by her mother, who, in spite of the poverty of their surroundings, shone like a gem. "She was a beautiful woman—glamorous—and had wonderful taste. She worked hard but she always took care of herself. And she *loved* shoes." The shoes that Helen most admired were her mother's collection of dress shoes with formidable 3-4 inch heels. Even as a child, she simply could not resist them.

"My mom got a call from my teacher when I was in middle school," Helen confesses. "My teacher told her: 'Helen comes to school wearing the most *amazing* shoes.' That was how my mom found out that I was taking her shoes and wearing them at school. I hid them in my locker and I learned how to walk in those heels at school."

Helen's mom gave her a sound scolding: "Do you know how hard I had to work to get those shoes!" she said. Helen remembers being contrite—but she was also entirely hooked. She vowed that the first thing she would do for herself when she 'made it'—when she had money—would be to buy herself some gorgeous shoes. "A woman in her beautiful shoes," she says, "knows that she belongs!"

My Own Experience

For me, the alternative universe offered by theater was the bright and shining star I wished upon. I was probably five or six when I saw my first professional theatrical performance. My parents took my sister and me to see *Holiday on Ice* in London for a special treat.

Although I had no particular desire to become an ice skater, how I loved those costumes that sparkled, shimmered and floated under the lights! I would give anything to live in that magical world, bringing such joy to people.

As my parents were determined to climb out of the post-war destruction that had laid waste to most of Europe, they worked hard and sought opportunities for a better life.

Working as servants on large private estates, they were eventually hired, via an agent in London, by wealthy Americans for private service and emigrated to the Hamptons on Long Island.

Most often servants in this line of work were childless. There were many married couples, both of whom worked in the 'Main House' but they rarely came with children. Children were noisy and unruly and simply did not fit into the manicured environment of a private estate.

But we were English and English children were known to be different from American children. We were used to being quiet; we had good manners; we never asked for seconds—or even firsts. We knew our place.

I spent my teens working alongside my mother in the Main House as a chambermaid. I grew up in that environment, learning from my mother—who was a master—to move without making a sound, to be in a room and disappear into the wallpaper.

I grew up, went to college, dropped out, got married and had a baby. I began working in downtown Washington DC, in the vast 'pink collar' landscape of corporate America, paying health insurance claims. I followed the rules, paid my bills on time and struggled to find meaning in my life. Riding the commuter bus home from work every night, I used to ask myself, "Is this all there is?"

In my 20s, I went back to school part time at night, determined to change my life. It took most of that decade—taking a class here, several more there, but I persevered. Under the strain, my marriage frayed and began to unravel as I began my hard-won senior year of college, and then broke apart for good. Two months later, a month after my 30th birthday, my father died suddenly of a heart attack.

I had followed the rules, tried to be responsible and yet my life had come to this. The decade of my 20s ended in ashes.

Helen's Guccis

For Helen as well, it looked as though her dreams of a better life would remain forever in the realm of fantasy. By the time she was 17, she was the mother of two children. But she had no intention of sitting on the sidelines of life.

"I was broke, with two kids, but I went to cosmetology school and started my own business when I was 18," she says.

As a teen, Helen suffered from *alopecia*—severe hair loss. Armed with her training in cosmetology, however, she experimented and eventually developed a non-surgical treatment for the condition. "I created a method that is now used worldwide," she says. "I have a passion to help women deal with this problem." Her dedication, she says, was inspired by her mother, for whom fashion and beauty were so important.

"I struggled as a mother with young kids, but I was never on welfare. I wasn't able to finish school at the time, but I went back and finished later. Addiction runs deep in my family, but I never took drugs or got messed up with alcohol."

Helen hung in there—although those dreams of the magical life she had glimpsed as a child were elusive.

Working hard and on her own for ten years, Helen finally saw her business thrive and her fortunes multiply. She was still very careful with her money, however, and conservative with her indulgences.

And then for her birthday one year, her sister sent her a pair of shoes—and not just any shoes, a pair of Guccis. Helen was overwhelmed. "She knows how much I love beautiful shoes, especially Guccis. As a young woman I longed to own a pair, but at the time I wouldn't even dream about spending that much on a pair of shoes. I'd admire these shoes in store windows and catalogs, and I'd tell my sister, 'One day I'll make enough money to afford my very own pair.' When she sent me those shoes, I felt I had received the biggest hug from her I could ever get, and I tell you, I never cried more."

My Top Hat

As for me, struggling with the loss of both my marriage and then my father, I was deep in my own despair, dragging myself to class in a fog. And then one day, when I happened to cut through the park on the way to class, I came upon a group of jugglers. They were doing incredible tricks with colorful balls and clubs and having such a wonderful time. I got entirely distracted, forgot about my class and stood entranced, watching them until they packed up and went off.

I went back the next day, unable to stay away. Not long after, I met up with Lindsay, one of the jugglers, and we became fast friends. He taught me how to juggle the basic three- ball cascade. We began hanging out together and after a few months, he invited me to come with him on an open-ended bicycle trip to New England. A bit of a counter-culture hippy, Lindsay did not own a car and was an experienced long distance bicyclist.

Had it been any other time in my life, I would have turned down his invitation. I had not been on a bicycle in years and open-ended adventures were a tad too 'irresponsible' for someone like me. But I had followed all the rules and had lost everything anyway. I decided I had nothing left to lose, and so, in my senior year of college, with that degree nearly within my grasp, I dropped out of school and went on the road.

And so we set off. We planned to earn our traveling money through street performing as we went—passing the hat for our daily bread.

Unfortunately, I was a disaster at first. I had spent my life being low-key and staying in the background, which were not the best traits for performing. Lindsay came up with a plan that he determined would break me out of my mold. I would take on the role of 'barker': it would be my job to draw the crowd. Frankly, I was terrified—beyond terrified. I tried to psych myself up for it. I asked myself, "What do I have to lose?" These were not people I knew or would ever see again. It was time to pluck up my courage, find my voice and come out of the shadows. It was my chance to become one of those magical performers I had seen so many years ago...if I could just get up the nerve!

And so I cheated. I felt compelled to find a prop, to have *something* to hold onto that would give me courage—just as Dumbo, the flying elephant, found his courage with his feather. In our performance gear was a battered pop-up top hat that we used to 'pass the hat' at the end of the shows. I loved the 'pop' sound that accompanied the action of flicking it open; I loved the simple drama in that act. And so I put that hat on, tapping it twice for good measure. All of a sudden, I could hear myself being the barker: "Step right up, ladies and gentlemen! The show is about to begin!"

"What Do Women Want?"
By Kim Addonizio

I want a red dress.
I want it flimsy and cheap,
I want it too tight, I want to wear it
until someone tears it off me.
I want it sleeveless and backless,
this dress, so no one has to guess
what's underneath. I want to walk down
the street past Thrifty's and the hardware store
with all those keys glittering in the window,
past Mr. and Mrs. Wong selling day-old
donuts in their café, past the Guerra brothers
slinging pigs from the truck and onto the dolly,
hoisting the slick snouts over their shoulders.
I want to walk like I'm the only
woman on earth and I can have my pick.
I want that red dress bad.
I want it to confirm
your worst fears about me,
to show you how little I care about you
or anything except what
I want. When I find it, I'll pull that garment
from its hanger like I'm choosing a body
to carry me into this world, through
the birth-cries and the love-cries too,
and I'll wear it like bones, like skin,
it'll be the goddamned
dress they bury me in.

It didn't happen overnight, but I grew into the role. Down the road, I added a colorful hatband, added some feathers and trinkets that I found as we traveled. I didn't feel like a silent partner: I *felt* like a performer, like a ringmaster. There was something about putting that hat on my head that made me feel differently. And when I took the hat off, I could quietly melt back into the crowd—perfect!

So that was me—the year I turned 30—standing on a street corner, doing something I could never have imagined myself doing: making a spectacle of myself in public. I was raised never to speak to strangers, never to raise my voice and *certainly*, never to draw attention to myself. But then I put on my top hat: "Oh baby—look at me now!"

For Helen, beautiful shoes were her props, the icon she carried in her heart. She, too, tried on the magic when she 'borrowed' her mother's shoes back in middle school—and eventually, she made that magic manifest in her own life.

"As we are working to become who we are," Helen says, "we should use every little thing that empowers us. My shoes are the reward I've given myself over the years as a hard-working woman who came from poverty, had two children by the time I was 17, and was expected to amount to nothing. As a young woman I'd admire the beauty and power of other women who were not 'in my shoes,' hoping one day I would get out of the projects and be just like them.

"When I could finally afford my first pair of Christian Louboutins, I realized I was becoming the woman I always knew I could be. I believe recognizing and owning one's personal power is one of the most important rites of passage any girl or woman can experience. Today I celebrate my life even as I realize that I could have ended up like my neighbors— either in jail or on the streets. And I celebrate who I am through my shoes and wardrobe."

Helen's shoes were definitely made for walking! She spends a lot of her time not only focusing on expanding her business but also giving back to her community and encouraging young people to follow their dreams as well.

All of our lives have times of ebb and flow. Just as we hope to move on down the road in style, we also need to honor our time to withdraw. Glad rags can help create our secure base as well as you will see in the next chapter.

No Place Like Home

Having the courage and the *chutzpah* to walk out the door often relies on having a sure sense of the opposite: knowing you have a safe and secure place to return to. It may not be a physical place—not be a house, perhaps not even be a country. The security of a physical place can be breeched. Someone can come into that space who makes you feel uncomfortable or threatened. But when you are able to create that place for yourself, within yourself, you will find that you can always 'go home.'

Jim

A few years ago, I designed and taught a community arts class called *Embracing Chaos*, which was basically a class in creativity, in learning to think outside the box. One of the assignments was to physically create an environment for someone or something. One of my students, a quiet, middle-aged man, came to class wearing his faded overalls, an old flannel shirt and a battered straw hat.

"What did you make for your environment, Jim?" I asked him. In response he stood up, spread out his arms and said, "This is it."

Seeing my confusion and the confusion of everyone else in the class, he explained, "These are the clothes I live in. These are the clothes that make me feel at home."

And he was absolutely right. He was at home when he was wearing his glad rags.

He could get dressed for work, walk out his door and face the world, knowing that when he came back he could take off his work clothes and put on those clothes that made him feel secure and 'at home.'

Creating Private Space

In many traditional cultures, a prayer shawl or blanket is used to create a private or sacred space— particularly in those cultures whose traditions arise from a nomadic way of living, or where the people have been displaced because of war or natural disaster.

In traditional nomadic cultures—as well as in modern refugee communities—communal living is the norm and creating private space is something that happens on the fly. Constructing a holy building isn't entirely practical if you are off wandering around the desert with herds of sheep or goats or if you are living in a temporary shelter.

I discovered this for myself as my own house has a 'revolving door'—adult children and grandchildren have moved back in and out a number of times over the course of the last decade. I have a relatively large family by modern standards—five children and now eight grandchildren. 'Empty Nesters' we are not, as our children have grown up and moved out, and then have periodically moved back in for a while. They are sometimes in the process of moving or going to school or ending a relationship and so come home for a few weeks, months or years.

A few years ago, my oldest daughter and her 18-month-old daughter relocated from several states away to be closer to the family fold. They lived with us for about nine months while my daughter found a job and got established in the new home state. The week she moved in, my youngest daughter, a third year college student, following the ending of a long-standing relationship, also moved back in.

Added to the mix was one of my young grandsons, who hung out with me while his mom attended classes and worked part time. At the same time, my job (full time newspaper editor) was in the process of being reorganized and I was switching to telecommuting. Hence, I was preparing to work full time from home and my workspace was stuffed with boxes of office supplies and records.

In the middle of all of this, my husband decided that it was time to rip out the living room floor and replace the sub-floor and carpeting to get rid of the terminal squeaks that we had endured for about for 20 years or so.

The couch was in the kitchen, chairs piled in the hall and other amorphous clutter from the living room was stashed in bedrooms and downstairs. I was awakened by daily hammering and had to carefully pick my way across the flooring joists to traverse the yawning holes that plunged all the way to the basement. And, of course, the daily business of life and editing and so forth was being squeezed in around the edges.

I am fairly laid back—but I confess—in the midst of the chaos, I felt more than a bit dismayed. I love my family; yet wondered, at the same time, how was I going to carve out a bit of personal space and attend to my own spiritual life and sanity. The answer was right under my nose.

I happened to be working on a press release, which included a photo of a group of Jewish clergywomen wearing *tallis,* traditional prayers shawls. Eureka! Of course! A prayer shawl! The ancient Hebrews were nomads. They moved as a group across trackless desert and wilderness. They were also invaded numerous times, their temples destroyed and the people forced into exile. Living a communal and often nomadic lifestyle, they used prayer shawls pulled over shoulders and head to create a personal temple in which to commune with God, a tradition that had remained a part of their religious observance down into modern times.

In the middle of my sprawling family tribe, looking for my little piece of spiritual real estate, I remembered a colorful lightweight Mexican blanket my mother  had given me and which I had stowed in a cedar chest for safekeeping. I pulled it out, wrapped myself in it and *viola!* My own personal temple where I could empty my chattering brain and open myself to the deep moving Mystery. It was a sweet experience.

Marla

Likewise, Marla, a columnist for a city newspaper, tells about a poncho she had stashed away in her

Isaac's Blessing
By Janet Eigner

When Isaac, a small, freckled boy
approaching seven, visits us for Family Camp,
playing pirate with his rubber sword,

sometimes he slumps in grief,
trudging along, his sacrifice and small violin
in hand, his palm over his chest,

saying, Mother is here
in my heart. Before he leaves for home,
we ask if he'd like a Jewish blessing.

Our grandson's handsome face ignites;
he chirps a rousing, yes, for a long life.
We unfold the prayer shawl,

its Hebrew letters silvering the spring light,
hold the white tallis above his head,
recite the blessing in its ancient language

and then the English, adding, for a long life.
Isaac complains, the tallis didn't
touch his head, so he didn't feel the blessing.

We lower its silken ceiling
to graze his dark hair,
repeat the prayer.

attic. It fulfilled a practical need in her life, but also connected her at a heart level to a dear uncle who had passed away.

When Marla broke her wrist after slipping and falling on the ice during a cold Midwest winter, she realized she had the perfect outer garment to wear with her awkward cast. She climbed into her attic and pulled out the alpaca poncho that was given to her by an uncle years ago when she was still a college student.

When Marla's Uncle Tony gave her the alpaca poncho from his native Peru, she was touched, even though it really wasn't her style. As an 80s college coed, she thought it entirely too 'funky' for her own stylish splendor.

"I wore it a few times," she says, "before relegating it to the back of my closet. It was too…hippie-ish and I was really not into that *boho* look."

The ethnic poncho was soft, thick alpaca wool in muted earth tones and, as she observed, although it had never gone out of style in 25 years, it had never really been *in* style this side of South America.

So why did she keep it? "I kept it for 15% practical and 85% sentimental reasons," she says. "I think it is an overwhelming female tendency," she says. "I'll bet that the majority of women have something in their closets that they have an emotional attachment to.

"Tony often traveled for business," she says. "When he was at home, though, he served as something of a badly needed father figure to me"—a role, she says, he was probably never even aware of.

Marla grew up, moved away, got busy with her life and career and, as often happens, they simply lost touch with one another.

And then, Marla heard through the family grapevine that Tony's health had suddenly declined and she was shocked and dismayed when she learned that he had died. She was planning to attend his memorial but the week before the event she fell on the ice and broke her wrist.

Since the memorial was to be held out of town and she suddenly could not drive, she did the next best thing. She climbed into her attic, retrieved the poncho and wrapped herself up in it.

Putting it on, she says, was like being enfolded in her dear Uncle Tony's comforting embrace. "It was like getting a big warm hug from him. I couldn't stop thinking about Tony and the effect that a person can have by offering a single act of kindness, or simply by being there."

Marla's poncho moved to the front of her closet and became the perfect choice of 'comfort clothing' while she was wearing a cast. "It's funny; I never would have thought of wearing it," she says. But she now found herself comforted and connected to the loving man who had given it to her many years before.

The added bonus for Marla was that she began getting a lot of compliments on her poncho, which she attributed to her own warm feelings about it as much as the appearance of the poncho itself.

My prayer shawl also provided a special connection to my mother. She had passed away the year before, having lived with me—via the revolving door—for three years prior to her death. She had been living in Texas for the previous 25 years and brought me the Mexican blanket because she loved bright, vibrant colors. This blanket was a deep purple, edged with red and yellow and she knew I would love it, too. I did love the colors but I had been storing the blanket in a cedar chest because I simply had no place to put it. When I was under duress, needing a place of quiet and calm, her blanket provided the tranquility that she herself so often embodied. How delightful that a garment can transmit that love and make it available to us long after the giver has passed away.

From all the stories shared by these women, it becomes obvious that glad rags are more than pieces of cloth with stitching, buttons and fastening. They connect us to dreams and memories, hopes and comfort; to our history, heritage and fancy. There is something lovely that happens when cloth meets skin.

PART II

Into the Marketplace

Sharing the Joy of Glad Rags

Some of the women I talked to have taken their own glad rags experience and run with it, creating more garments for the delight or comfort of others. These resourceful women began businesses to sell their handiwork, as did Brenda with her HugWraps. Others, like Suzelle, developed workshops to teach others how to make their own.

Most of the women were initially motivated by their own personal 'need' and passion. Based on how they felt, as well as positive feedback they received, these women understood they had stumbled upon something valuable to them personally that might have appeal for others as well.

Most of these women still have day jobs and deal with the challenges of the work-a-day world like everybody else. The satisfaction they find in creating and sharing the glad rags experience, however, spreads the joy around. And anything that adds a measure of joy to life on the planet is a thing to be celebrated!

Time and time again, these artists and craftswomen speak of the stories that get shared around this piece of clothing—this wrap, that hat, those gloves - and so it builds community, based on a common experience of putting on a piece of clothing. Dressing is an activity shared by everyone.

Yet another value of putting on your glad rags is that as you feel empowered and happier, you come to understand that you have plenty of positive 'juice' to share with others. And that is a transforming experience worth exploring.

7

Tammy—Red Panty Designs

Tammy designs clothing exclusively for the generously proportioned woman and sells them on *Etsy*, a worldwide, web-based marketplace where craftspeople can sell their handmade products; as well in boutiques. "I design for the 'real sized' woman," she says. Her designs are delightful examples of 'up-cycling'—doing recycling one better by creating new garments using fabric and embellishments from several others. She says the impetus for creating her clothing line was a case of simply "being selfish."

"I wanted clothing that was unique, comfortable, fancy, fun or flirty. I just couldn't find gorgeous clothing 'off the rack' that fit me well. There were no real options for women in sizes over 14."

Tammy had always sewn, came from a family of sewers and was the go-to person for fabulous Halloween and school play costumes. Her designer's eye and love of crafting came to the fore the spring she was looking for an Easter outfit.

She went in search of a linen dress but because of the way they were designed or cut, all the dresses she tried on were tent-like and unflattering. "I looked like a colored Easter egg," she said.

She went to a resale shop, found some skirts and tops she liked and then did the unthinkable: took scissors to dresses and skirts from well-known labels and reassembled them into something unique. She focused particularly on the drape, the flow of the garment, to ensure it was both comfortable and flattering.

"It was kind of scary at first," she admits. "I had to ask myself, 'Do I really want to do this?'" But after that first cut, she never looked back. "I go to Goodwill all the time; I am always looking for something to cut up.

"I love to sit in front of the TV with a stack of clothes and my big scissors," she says. "I cut out zippers, buttons, hook and eyes, waist bands and put them all in the appropriate jars. I 'fussy cut' everything and that prepping takes the longest. I want those details—a button line or a pocket, for instance—to fall in a particular place."

Her earliest efforts were simply a way to create clothes for herself that were both unique and flattering—but she was soon creating unique clothing for sale. Tammy wanted to create clothing that generously sized women would love and there were a lot of other women who shared her desire.

"I was at The Frame Shop (a store that carries her designs) and we were set up for the Arts Festival one year," Tammy says. "A woman came into the shop, then took several of my dresses into the changing room. She tried on one, put that aside. Then she tried on another, put that one aside. But when she tried that third dress on, she ran right through the store and out into the street and twirled around for her companions. When I make something for myself, *that* is exactly how I want to feel about it!"

Tammy's 'day job' is working as the curator for a university art museum in a college town, and it was during her tenure at the museum that the name for her clothing line emerged. "I was co-curator for a show at the museum and as often happens, friction arose with some co-workers. We were disagreeing about details of the show and it was going back and forth. I felt like I wasn't being listened to, that my opinion wasn't being respected. Then I just got to that point where I had had enough! In great indignation, I said to myself, 'I don't have to take this! I am wearing my red panties!'"

"I love red panties," she says, laughing, "because strong, confident women wear red panties! Someone like my mother, for instance, would *never* have worn red panties." Tammy also sports a streak of purple hair, something else her mother would never do!

Tammy creates other fiber art works, and red panties showed up repeatedly as a design motif in later art quilts that she made. A fellow quilt maker took note and identified the red panties as Tammy's 'personal icon.' It only made sense to use Red Panties as the name for her sassy clothing line.

"What was funny," she says, "after I launched the clothing line, all kinds of women began telling me about their 'red panty' experiences; it seems like almost everyone has a red panty story to share!"

8

Suzelle—Hat Theology

Suzelle has always loved hats. She came from a family who loved hats. "My grandmother was a real hat lady," she says. "Whenever she was unhappy— my mother says—she would bring home a hat. She apparently worked at a fancy women's boutique in Pontiac, Michigan, where she bought some fabulous hats.

"And I remember always getting Easter hats and gloves growing up. I had one that was a yellow straw hat with a daisy on it— I loved it!"

Suzelle's sisters and her father also love hats. One of her sisters lives in New Orleans and makes outrageous Mardi Gras headwear for friends and family.

Growing up and into a career in the corporate world, Suzelle recalls working in the PR department of an insurance company. At the conclusion of one particular project, she made the team whimsical hats out of paper, which were an instant success. They all wore their hats out for a celebratory meal. That experience prompted her to start making wild 'art hats' out of paper, especially from recycled posters and other items that would have otherwise ended up in the trash bin. She even sold a few at a local craft fair one holiday season.

When she subsequently entered seminary, Suzelle found working with hats to be an effective way of processing all the material she was studying. "Creating hats was a useful way to help me think outside the box," she says. "They were whimsical, yet so powerful. In a course on the roots and art of Jewish spirituality I discovered that, for me, sacred space was the space defined, refined, protected, projected—celebrated—by a hat. So the hats began to express some very serious spiritual issues and ideas."

Suzelle developed 'Hat Theology' workshops that she taught at church camps and retreats. The purpose of the workshops, she says, was to "invite participants to depict what they hold most sacred—on hats…" She encouraged them to "…create a soul hat, a spirit hat: put your soul on your hat!"

"It was wonderful to listen to them tell their hats' stories," she says. "A theological hat, when worn, can connect us with the unexpressed aspects of ourselves and our souls. Like a ceremonial headdress, it can transform the wearer into a deity."

As she moved into active ministry, Suzelle continued to create her hats. "I took my first and only serious millinery workshop from Seattle milliner, Izzie Lewis, during the time I was serving my first congregation in Bremerton, Washington," she says. "I kept making hats during that time as a way to seek balance between my work and my personal life."

She had the first gallery show of her hats in Bremerton in 1999, and they were part of a show with other milliners at Bumbershoot, Seattle's biggest arts festival, a few years later. When she moved to Wisconsin to serve a larger congregation, she asked to have her hats shown in the church's art gallery. "All the proceeds from the show went to fund an anti-racism, anti-oppression camp for teens," she says. "It was an interesting way to connect my artwork with my values and help my congregation make that connection as well." Serving a larger congregation and parenting her daughter have meant less time for hat making, but Suzelle usually has one or two hats 'in process' in her art room. "It's something I work on when I have time—it still lights up my soul," she says.

Fifteen years later, she still teaches hat making—although these days the workshops have been a bit more frivolous. "I teach people to make wild, fabulous cocktail hats," she says. "It is so interesting to see what people do. Hats are not usually worn 'just for fun' and people are often afraid of being outrageous."

Under her expert and infectious enthusiasm, however, the women who take her workshops often appear at special events and service auctions sporting their creations. They are disciples in Rev. Suzelle's army of believers: wearing hats is good, meaningful fun—a party on your head, and a boost for the spirit!

9

Linda—Whimseywear

After a difficult mid-life divorce, Linda bought herself a tiny cabin in the mountains of Northern California and began rebuilding her life. She painted her cabin with rainbow stripes and now creates whimsical furnishings and clothing as the mood strikes her.

She supports herself as a manicurist, where she gets to play with color and design on a daily basis. In younger days, Linda says she spent a lot of her time worried about what other people would think. But she always had a colorful fantasy life.

"At this point in my life, I am exploring all the fun I missed when I was younger," she says. "Now, I simply try things to see how they work out. I am allowing the gypsy in me to come out at last."

The clothes she wears—particularly up-cycled sweater-coats, hats and hand warmers—are an expression of her wide-open, adventurous spirit. She buys bags of sweaters, skirts and dresses—usually from thrift stores—and transforms them into whimsical garments, crazy quilts of color and pattern. Even though Linda maintains an *Etsy* shop and Facebook page dedicated to her designs, most of her creations, she says, are purchased 'off her body.'

"I will be walking down the street in the village where I live and people will simply walk up to me and want to buy my coat or hat" she says.

The clothes she creates are manifestation of a vibrant life energy that holds great appeal for many people. That life energy was in full force when, on a whim, she decided to visit Scotland. "I bought a plane ticket with no bookings or reservations—no particular plan in place, other than to spend a month or so over there."

She is not of Scottish heritage nor had any particular ties to Scotland other than having read some historical fiction that was set there. "I'm Danish," she says, "a Viking. I went entirely on faith."

Once there, she bought a train pass and cast about for a short while. "Then I decided I'd better sign up for a tour so I didn't miss everything!" she says. She signed up for a tour of the Isle of Wight." I struck up a conversation with the tour guide and the next thing I knew, she invited me to come live with her for a month, rent free, and she would make sure I saw Scotland! We went to the Orkneys, the Outer Hebrides and many other places I had only read about.

"It was like magic," she says. "From that experience, I learned I could trust in myself and my decisions—that I could trust in the Universe, something I never would have believed in my younger days."

Linda came home with some lovely memories, as well as a whole spate of inspiration for new designs. Currently she is playing with clothing and design elements from the Scottish Highlands—tribal belly dance, gypsy and steam punk culture—and having a blast. She might be a late bloomer, but Linda has blossomed into a vibrant, colorful flower.

10

Rae—Dream Hats

Rae is a surgical nurse at The Ohio State University, James Cancer Center. She is also the designer and creative force behind Dream Hats, colorful and comfortable scrub hats that are hand made by volunteers and given to cancer patients.

"I work in the operating room, so we have to wear surgical scrubs, including hats" says Rae. "You can buy them online, but I have always enjoyed sewing, so I decided to make some hats. Initially I made them for myself out of colorful fabric; it was about the only way to be an individual as part of the surgical team. Then I made them for other members of my staff as a morale booster for the patients we were treating."

It wasn't long before the colorful scrub hats caught the attention of other nurses and health care providers, and they wondered if Rae might make them hats as well. She was happy enough to oblige.

"It is part of the staff responsibility to interview patients in pre-op and all of the staff members—

nurses, anesthesiologists, radiologists—were wearing colorful hats.

"There was a patient, a 22-year old student nurse, who came in for a biopsy of a lump in her breast. We were talking her through the various possibilities and options should that diagnosis prove positive. Although she had some anxieties about the surgical procedure, her biggest fear was the prospect of losing her hair if she had to go through chemo. And then she admired our hats. 'Where can I get a hat like that if I have to go through chemo?' she asked me. 'I might look into purchasing some for myself…just in case.'

"I just happened to have some of the hats in my locker that I had made for staff members," says Rae. "I went and got one and gave it to her."

After that experience, Rae switched her focus. "Initially, I just made them and gave them to our patients; but pretty soon, other patients in other departments began requesting them as well. Patients told me that while they were lying on the table, the hats gave them something cheerful 'to look up to.'

"Nurses began taking names and emails of those requesting hats, and I began getting these long lists of people. I was spending all my time trying to contact people through email, so I finally got permission to make hats and simply leave them here at the hospital to be distributed as needed."

As demand for Dream Hats mushroomed, Rae wondered how she was ever going to keep up with her hat production. But the enthusiasm for making Dream Hats had spread to the whole staff; it eventually spread to the whole community.

Volunteers staged fundraisers and Rae was soon busily buying fabric. "I took money and coupons in hand and bought as much fabric and remnants that I could manage. Then I brought all the fabric to an OR (operating room) staff meeting along with the pattern I had used to make them and gave everyone a lesson in how to cut out the Dream Hat."

Volunteer groups from the community signed up to help, and Rae was soon coordinating assembly lines that would have made Henry Ford proud. She had new recruits busily cutting out hat pieces, and before too long the piles of hat pieces were ready to be sewn together and bagged.

Eventually, she joined forces with another volunteer group serving the hospital and they had access to a sewing studio. "I met the coordinator," says Rae, "and she offered us space in her studio. That space is equipped with sewing machines and ironing boards. So we put up signs in the OR inviting anyone who wanted to help."

Rae set up times and taught volunteers how to sew. "At the first session we had maybe 15-20 people. Some knew the basics of sewing but didn't know how to make hats. By the end of the session, we had everyone sewing.

"We meet once a month and make the hats assembly line style. We have volunteers of all ages and abilities and there are many tasks to do, like cutting, sewing, ironing, putting in elastic and packing. Many of the volunteers come from the hospital and many others come from the community. It depends on the numbers that show up, but on any given Saturday, we might complete 100-125 hats. Everything has just fallen into place."

At this point in time, over 3,000 hats have been created by volunteer labor. Dream Hats have found their way out of Ohio and across the country. Members of Rae's extended family who have battled with breast cancer have found comfort in Dream Hats as well. Rae says many cancer survivors who have worn the hats have provided valuable feedback about preferred fabric and styles as she continues to refine the designs. Rae and her Dream Team hope the program will expand to involve other health and hospital facilities in the area.

It all began with one woman and one pair of hands with a desire to bring a bit of cheer into the lives of cancer patients. Now made by many hands and blessed by many hearts, Dream Hats continue to bring comfort and joy to many.

Tina—Tina's Tiaras

Tina intends to prove her mother wrong.

"My mother always told me: 'Tina, you can't expect to have fun all the time, because if that is what you think, you are going to be disappointed.'" Tina just laughs and keeps on making tiaras.

Tina's Tiaras are not your usual, beauty queen items with rhinestones and hair combs. Tina lets her wild child out to play as she creates tiaras in a profusion of colors and shapes, made from bent wire, colorful beads, jewels and, when requested, colored lights. "I especially like lights for camping," she says. "The lights are rice-sized LEDs with a small battery pack that tucks behind your ear. They come in pink, blue, white, red or purple.

"Tiaras are fun to wear," she says. "It's what I want to do all the time: find the fun."

Tina makes tiaras part time and hopes eventually to work up to full time. But for right now, she lives 'in the middle of nowhere' and commutes to her 'day job' as an intervention specialist working with at-risk preschoolers in southern Ohio.

She credits her community of women friends for providing the inspiration to take her tiara-making hobby to the next level as a business. "When we first became friends we were all single. We loved dressing up! We used to buy party dresses at the thrift store and host 'inappropriate cocktail parties.' And then we got married and had kids; we went back to school, worked really hard. These women—my friends—are powerful women, brave women, who also happen to have these fun alter egos. And you know, if you seriously want that kind of fun in your life, you have to be into it— you have to invest in it."

Tiaras, Tina says, have particular power in that respect. "Tiaras touch everyone; they are magic. They make a huge difference in people's lives. It is amazing to me that so many people who have bought my tiaras come back and tell me their stories: how my tiaras have helped them deal with difficult things like breast cancer; how the tiaras make the most mundane things bearable—like taxes or rush hour traffic.

"I keep a tiara on the dashboard of my car, for 'emergencies,'" she says. "I wear them for housework, parties and shows; I wear them when I have my annual mammogram; I wore one when I turned 50 and had to endure the most invasive procedure imaginable, a colonoscopy. The medical staff notice you and they remember you, to be sure!"

Tina scored her first 'serious' tiara on eBay. "I originally had a tiny tiara that I wore around the house. I bought it at a thrift store and it was small and easy to ignore. But when I wore it around my girlfriends, they all wanted one, so we all ended up with rhinestone tiaras that we ran in and bought at Yankee Trader, a huge party and novelty store in the city, while my friend Robin circled the block in her van."

Tina soon decided that not just any old tiara would do for her, so she went on a quest for her own special headpiece. "I became convinced that I needed the biggest one, since the whole tiara thing was my idea," she says. She turned to the biggest marketplace of all: eBay. "I had measured everyone else's tiara first, so when I got on eBay, I knew it needed to be more than 4.5 inches tall. I searched for months.

"Finally, while visiting my sister in Oregon, I found one listed," says Tina. "It had curved spirals with points coming out of the top all around. I loved it right away. I remember the way my sister looked at me while I hooted and shrieked all over her kitchen. It was waiting at my house when I returned and I was thrilled.

"From that point on, when we all went out together; there was no mistaking who was in charge! I had the biggest, tallest bling-iest tiara in the group. I wore it on bad days at work and when I was driving in the car.

"I think the defining point for the whole tiara rite came when we started wearing our tiaras camping. We became known as the Divas and the name still sticks to us today. We reveled in our new title and printed T-shirts for ourselves," she says. "Young women began following behind us, wanting advice on how they, too, could move through the world while keeping a sense of humor, passion and love."

It wasn't long after that Tina moved from consumer to creator. "I started making tiaras after one of the Divas bought a wire and beaded tiara online. It was amazingly fabulous and even larger than mine! It was just made from beads and wire; how hard could it be to make my own? We tried to make some while camping. They started out fabulous, but as the day went on and the vodka flowed, they became increasingly 'camp-craft' quality. But I was determined to make a beautiful tiara on my own so I bought more wire and worked at it until I produced one that made me happy.

"I made more for Christmas presents and all of the recipients suggested that we get together and make them and try to get a booth for Comfest, an annual community arts festival. We met every Sunday for almost a year for the purpose of making tiaras; applied and got into the show. We had no money for a booth so we went to Walmart, picked all our gear out and then returned it after the show. I loved it! I kept at it and learned how the show circuit worked, made friends with other artists, got into a gallery and it has snowballed from there."

Tina has become a sought-after vendor at craft fairs and peddles her magical head gear as well on Facebook and through her website.

Tina also donates tiaras as the need arises. When a customer purchased a tiara for a young niece undergoing cancer treatment, Tina donated enough tiaras for the whole ward. And when Tina's SO ("significant other") was undergoing major surgery, she took a batch of sparkly tiaras along and handed them out to all the scrub and surgical nurses. "Particularly in a hospital setting, folks need something fun, something to lift their spirits" she says. And tiaras are nothing if not fun.

12

Brenda—HugWraps Go International

"If I had just come up with this design to make money, to have a business," says Brenda, "I don't think it would have caught on the same way. But there is the emotional connection of one cancer patient making this for another cancer patient. And those people totally get why I made these wraps. They think: 'she knows what I am going through.' Sewing these was the best therapy for me, especially as I got on a mission to help other patients."

After Brenda donated her personal stash of HugWraps to her oncologist's office, people soon began contacting her about purchasing further wraps for themselves or for their loved ones. Initially, she made them for free or for donations, but quickly realized she would not be able to afford her charitable activity in light of the mushrooming demand. She was determined to continue, however, and eventually grew her HugWraps into a full time business. "Each of the HugWraps is still custom made," she says, "according to measurements and the openings needed for each person's treatment. They are time intensive but since they are custom fitted, I still make them myself."

She did get a boost from an unexpected source, however. "There is a TV show, *George to the Rescue,* where they do renovations for a non-profit, and he chose me! They came in and renovated my bedroom-office and then outfitted a spare bedroom with shelves for storage."

Brenda's story has been shared through many articles and interviews, and the HugWraps have been sent all over the country as well as to Poland, Australia and the UK. She often travels to speak at hospitals and cancer wards. "I have made HugWraps for children as well," she says. "After parents remarked how much the children really liked the colorful fabric, I began making other things for the kids to brighten their stay—like pillowcases, lap blankets and IV pole covers. When I visit pediatric cancer wards, I give these 'extras' away to the children. I use leftover material from the HugWraps or other fabric that people donate. They are a quick sewing project and there are a couple of quilting clubs that help me out."

After a lengthy application process, she was finally approved as a 501c3—a non-profit business. "I would love to get corporate or medical sponsorship," she says, "but have not been able to get anything so far. It is a constant ongoing struggle, but I keep going. It takes patience but I feel like it is what I am supposed to do."

13

Renna—Hats, a Self-narrative

Renna is not a professional artist, but she enjoys crafting things for her own enjoyment as well as to give to friends. Knitting is a favorite activity, as is birding and playing music. Renna is Jewish, a psychotherapist and spiritual advisor. While hats are not required of Jewish women in synagogue—unless they are Orthodox and thereby required to cover hair after marriage—many Jewish women now follow the practice.

"I wear hats on Shabbat when I'm at Torah study; and whenever I am in synagogue. I don't wear them all the time, though I often would like to. It would just represent such an identity change (for my patients, my husband, myself) that I keep the reverence part of my internal covenant and wear it whenever I want that covenant to feel more public.

"When did I begin to wear hats as a beloved accessory? As little children we wore hats our Mom knitted; as we got older we were given new hats every spring, little affairs with ribbons and flowers. I must have loved the feeling of wearing them, because I began to wear hats again as an adult—high fashioned black ones with big brims when I was younger—then as I got older I added berets, straw sunhats, quirkily shaped hats, stylish fleece ones with velour flowers for the winter, cotton hats with malleable brims for hiking or with summer clothes and baseball style caps with names of bird refuges on them or my favorite: my NY Yankees cap.

"I love the way that hats contribute something unique to the way we look. I think it takes confidence and whimsy to play with form and shape—to know enough about the heft of your head, the look of your face and the overall impression you make, to incorporate a hat into your self-image.

"Hats create a self-narrative into which the rest of your appearance fits. Some hats speak about vulnerability, others about sensuality and sex, others cuteness, others elegance; for some it completely defines a spiritual path or a culture. When I wear my cowboy hat, I am remembering the deserts I have traveled and my desert ancestors.

"Hats help us humans to exist in a world of climatological extremes. I always wear hats when I bird or hike. I don't want to worry about what my hair looks like—if it's frizzing up from the fog—and I certainly don't want to have to fuss with it when we're getting up at 4 a.m. to catch the birds when they are just coming back to life. It gives me control over the way the world comes at me: extra warmth, protection from the wind and rain and relief from the heat.

"And, ultimately, hats are fun. They are fun to knit and crochet, to pick up and throw on your head as you're passing through the hat section, with a quick glance in the mirror, prompting us to wonder: 'Who am I now?'"

Renna poses an interesting question: "Who am I now?" Practicing real life or trying on alternative lives is the power that resides in our exploration of glad rags. Who you are now *is entirely up to you*!

PART III

The Changing Room

14

Glad Rags Mighty and Mundane

If you look back at the stories you have just read, you will find a simple, surprising thread that runs through every experience: a feeling of fun, delight and even a giddy sense of absurdity in the face of challenges, both mundane and overwhelming. Very often, the glad rags experience is a game-changer and is coupled with a yelp of delight, a laugh out loud or simply a slow-spreading smile of satisfaction.

When was the last time you heard someone talk about having 'fun' with Parkinson's Disease? Judy put on a loud and colorful jacket that helped her imagine how to actively engage with a very scary disease. It lifted her spirits, engaged her sense of play as well as shored up her courage as she began to deal with the reality of her life in the aftermath of her daunting diagnosis. Her playful spirit, embodied by 'da Coat is both inspiring and infectious. People want to hang out with her, put on her coat, share her journey and do whatever they can to help her "endure for the cure".

Have you ever considered that changing the kind of underwear you are wearing, like Amy did, might have a huge impact on how successful you are in your business? How silly is that? (And didn't you just smile even thinking about it?)

How about Tina's example: Could you picture yourself getting a colonoscopy in a sparkly tiara? How would you feel sailing into your oncology appointment, like Brenda did, in a stunning hospital gown that drew gasps of admiration from the other patients?

All of a sudden, the thing that terrifies you, that makes you want to shrink away and hide from the world, is made manageable. You can step out, engage the world and laugh in the face of fears, or smile, even through your tears.

There are a lot of other phrases we use when talking about clothing—'dressing for success,' wearing a 'power suit' or being on the 'cutting edge' of fashion—that don't tend to make us smile—quite the contrary! When faced with a threatening or challenging situation, our bodies gear up for the 'fight or flight' response: breathing becomes shallow, muscles tense, blood flow increases to our hands. Other thoughts and responses take a backseat as our bodies shift into survival mode.

And don't get me wrong; there are times when that kind of mind-set is appropriate for the situation. Many of the women who have shared their glad rags experiences function quite effectively in the real world. They are teachers and business executives, ministers, reporters, counselors and nurses. They 'dress for success' in their professional realm; they know how to fit into the workaday world.

The glad rags experience isn't like that. It doesn't make you edgy and tense; glad rags make you feel… well…glad, of course! You feel happy, energized and upbeat: you access the 'rest and digest' mode.

Putting on your glad rags is like a great big exhale…aaaaahhhhhhhh…and feeling fine inside your skin. When you feel good about *you,* most often you also feel good about yourself in connection with others 'out there.'

Tina creates fun tiaras but there is also a pair of remarkable boots in her story.

"My mother was a majorette in high school," says Tina. "When I was growing up, there were all these photos around our house of my mother in her outfit, looking really beautiful in those white majorette boots." Tina also came into her teens in the '70s when fashion took a decidedly 'mod' turn and white Go-Go Boots were the hot item. "Go-Go Boots were in style," she says, "and I *really* wanted them—but I wasn't allowed to have any."

Nevertheless, the vision of those boots stuck in Tina's head. "A few years later, I was managing a vintage clothing store and a pair of those white boots came in. They were a little bit too big but I didn't care. The moment I put them on, I just felt differently. I wore them everywhere—and I still have them. Back in the day, when I was getting dressed to go to a party, friends would literally call me up to ask me if I were wearing them that night. Other friends would ask to borrow them. They were welcome wherever they went and they got passed around quite a bit!"

When your purpose in dressing for success is to get 'the edge' over your rivals, you certainly aren't inclined to share— if for no other reason than you might just lose your advantage! But the glad rag experience leads to a happy place and generosity is a common by-product.

Judy regularly lends out 'da Coat to others who tap into its pizzazz in order to advocate and educate about Parkinsons' Disease. She does not hoard it and use it only to further her own reputation. 'Da Coat has climbed Mt. Everest and marched in Central Park; 'da Coat has even stopped by my house to spread its magic around!

When Helen was finally successful in her beauty-based business, she celebrated that success by walking out into her community—in her kick-ass designer high heel shoes, thank you very much!—to inspire other youngsters to follow their dreams. When Amy's Super Girl underpants helped her fly to the top of her skin care sales force, she wasted no time extending a helping hand to other women who were struggling to stay aloft.

What Is It About Those Glad Rags?

What is it that is so transforming about such a seemingly trivial thing as putting on a pair of boots or a jacket? Why does that physical action trigger a psychological/emotional response?

Social scientists refer to this experience as 'embodied cognition.' When psychologist William James was considering the mind-body connection in 1884, he discovered that one's 'state of mind'—how we feel about something—is mirrored in bodily expression or behavior. If we are depressed, for instance, our body manifests depression physically. We all know that feeling, I am sure! Our shoulders slump, we move slowly and laboriously, hang our head—and we sigh a lot, "ho hum."

Needless to say, James also discovered that the reverse was true, as demonstrated in Kate's situation.

She was feeling dispirited, struggling to keep mind and body together as she dealt with the relentless mud that surrounded her homestead. When she encountered her jacket, however, it immediately changed her state of mind. The jacket was so beautiful in her sight that it took her breath away and gave her hope again.

When you physically encounter something delightful, something that makes you smile, it changes your state of mind. Your mind releases endorphins—the 'happy' hormone—and you immediately perk up. Research into brain chemistry has also shown that when we are in this happy state, we feel much more generous and connected to other people.

When we are children, during our imaginative play, we do not analyze everything. We respond directly, physically. We don't think about it, we simply do it. We put on a cape and become a fairy queen or super heroine, and there is no doubt or question in our minds—the act of putting on a cape *makes* us a fairy queen. Even when that cynical older brother comes walking through and says, "That's not a cape; it's just a stupid pillow case," we ignore him. What does he know? We don't 'think'; we *know* with our whole body and soul.

Our grown up brains have been busy for years, gathering and storing away all sorts of information and forming opinions to better guide our adult behavior. But let's face it, some of that stored information, that baggage in your brain, might be incomplete, outdated or just plain wrong. How do you get past that know-it-all gatekeeper? You put your glad rags on, baby; you can't simply *think* about it—you have to *put your glad rags on.*

As Barbara was facing the great unknown of menopause, the chatter in her mind made her feel anxious and afraid. Not knowing what to expect, her mind provided plenty of worst-case scenarios, drawn from conversations she had heard or articles she had read. The brain gathered all that information and served up a pessimistic picture of her future.

However, stored in her brain as well was a memory of a time, when, as a child, she felt powerful and optimistic. In that memory, the feeling was tied directly to a pair of red cowgirl boots, a gift from God and to her mind, the answer to a prayer.

She remembered the physical sensations of that day: the excitement at seeing the boots, the smell of the leather, the smoothness of the interior as her feet slid into the boots, and the dazzling smile that broke across her face as a result.

When she went in search of a pair of boots for her adult self, her mind tried to direct her search based on current data; considerations of cost and practicality elbowed their way to the front. But her touchstone was that physical response: a full body smile from childhood that lit up her face when she put on the red boots. And when she found her grown up glad rags—the buffalo hide boots—and slipped them on, the effect was immediate. It didn't come from a rational place; it came directly from her skin. The clincher? She spontaneously broke into that radiant smile. Embodied cognition: her body guided her to the place that her adult mind had dismissed as 'kid stuff.'

For Barbara, boots were an *icon*, something we are familiar with on our computer desktops. When we click the icon, we access our whole file. When Barbara puts on her buffalo hide boots, she accesses her reimagined and powerful self.

Syd and Jasey

I recently was told a story about how dressing up and playing with glad rags actually saved a marriage. I had known this couple for years and would never have guessed the dramatic role that glad rags has played in their lives.

Syd and Jasey started dating in middle school and they were a dedicated couple from then on. They grew up together, went off to college, got married, bought a house and prepared to start a family. They were a storybook couple and everything was rolling along smoothly—until it wasn't. Syd became increasingly dismayed, as month after month, year after year, she was unable to conceive. She felt entirely betrayed by her body.

"We went through fertility counseling and sex stopped being fun," says Syd. "The focus was on 'baby making' and I was a total failure. I had to deal with this body that was not working correctly. It created a real crisis in our marriage; I couldn't think about sex in terms of pleasing my husband. I suffered from a huge loss of self-esteem and battled with depression."

When cysts were discovered on one of her ovaries and the doctor scheduled her for surgery, Syd's reaction was swift. "I told him to just go ahead and take them both out," she says. "I was so angry and felt so betrayed by my body I think I just wanted to punish myself. I was just too angry to even think about it. I didn't understand the working of my body and why it had let me down."

What was done was done and Syd and Jasey moved on together. They were both busy with teaching careers and as youth group leaders. They were able to adopt two beautiful babies who greatly enriched their lives and later adopted two teen-aged girls. Over the years, they provided temporary shelter for many other young people as well. Their house and family was a haven. From the outside, they were still a perfect couple, successful and fulfilled.

But Syd carried an unhealed wound that would manifest itself from time to time in bouts of deep depression. Taking anti-depressants enabled her to function but created other problems that further affected her self-esteem.

"I had a 20 pound weight gain from taking Prozac," she says. "I just couldn't get out from under the vicious cycle. I did not feel the least bit attractive or seductive."

For his part, Jasey continued to love and desire Syd, but it made little impact. "Syd has always been a beautiful woman," he says. "I always thought she was gorgeous. But she was at war with her body and I was a civilian casualty."

Jasey had been a highly successful teacher; in his spare time, he is also been a popular rock musician. He is a talented and charismatic performer and never lacked for female admirers. It had never been an issue in their younger days, particularly as Syd often accompanied him on gigs. But as they got older and Syd stayed home more and more, trouble that had been simmering for years finally boiled over. It came to a head during a seemingly trivial argument over high heel shoes.

"He wanted to know why I wouldn't consider wearing high heel shoes," Syd says. "I was floored."

As it turned out, there was another woman in the picture. Syd finally came face to face with the possibility that she might actually lose her husband. "When you are hurting, as I had been for a long time, you only think of yourself. I realized that I would have to fight to get him back—and that included learning how to be a good sexual partner."

A friend shared a bit of wisdom that became the rallying cry for Syd. "Coe said to me 'you will never be younger and never be more beautiful than you are right now. You should work with that, accentuate that.' And that was what I decided to do."

Although Syd is indeed a striking woman, standing at 5'8" with energetic brown hair and a sprinkling of freckles across her nose, she had never considered herself attractive. But now she began to focus on her appearance. She adopted a healthier diet and dedicated herself to a regular exercise regime. "I began to look better, had more energy and as I felt better, I also started getting compliments on how I looked."

Emboldened, Syd took it to the next level. She walked into the kitchen where Jasey was having his

morning coffee, slid a lingerie catalogue across the table and said, "Dress me."

Needless to say, Jasey did not need to be asked twice. He was an enthusiastic partner in this game. Together they embarked on a playful quest, acquiring a fun and seductive wardrobe for their intimate moments. "We played," says Syd. " I got to play dress up in sexy clothing, something I had never done before." They found *bustiers* and lacy bras; low cut tops and saucy short skirts. They purchased high heels, long boots and leather pants—in short, they had a ball. "It entirely changed the playing field," she says. "It helped to set the mood, it helped me feel sexy. It enhanced a part of me that had never been accessed before."

Their sexy wardrobe was only for their bedroom, in the privacy of their own home—their 'secret garden.' But one year they went to Canada on vacation and Syd decided to pack a short leather skirt and jacket along with long black boots.

"I thought, 'Why not? No one is going to know me there.'"

In the hotel, Syd put on her leather outfit and they set out on a walk. "I became aware that there was a woman who seemed to be following us; she was right behind us," she says. "Then she stepped out to go past us, turned around and walked backwards so she was facing us. She looked at me and she said, 'You are so beautiful!'"

Jasey was entirely proud of his gorgeous wife, and Syd has never felt quite the same about herself again.

Come Out to Play!

Playtime is every bit as important for grownups as it is for children. It helps us recover those parts of ourselves that we have lost or have hidden away.

We have looked at the playful aspect of glad rags and how playfulness and delight energizes us. The other thread that runs through all these stories is self-care and compassion. All of these women acted on their own behalf to give themselves something that they really needed in their lives at that point in time.

To seek out and put on something that speaks to you is a radical act in itself—a small and seemingly insignificant choice—but a radical act nonetheless. It is a first step in truly caring for and loving yourself. Every time you take a small step forward in your own behalf—choosing something that makes a difference to you, and you alone—you are actively engaged in your journey, and every subsequent step in creating the kind of life that you have always wanted becomes easier.

Maybe you, like many of the women in this book, are standing at the crossroads knowing you have to do *something* in response to your own crisis of body or soul. Maybe you have an ache that won't go away and wish you could do *something* that would ease that pain. Maybe you have been zonked by a curve ball that you never saw coming. Maybe you know all about the 'wants' and the 'shoulds' but are really struggling with the 'how.' I expect if this is your struggle, you are saying to yourself, "Well, that's easy to *say*…but not so easy to *do*." And I hear you. That was my experience as well; it wasn't that I didn't want to—I simply didn't know how to get past my fear.

And then I put on a pop-up top hat and stepped out of the shadows. Boom! I became a circus.

As I have pointed out earlier, glad rags are specific to each person and their particular journey. The task thus becomes a personal quest. You have to find your own 'best clothes'; you have to find the glad rags that speak to you and you have to put them on.

So what are you waiting for? Let's get a few 'playful' considerations in place to help set the mood and then let's go shopping for the 'real' you.

Emily Dickinson and Elvis Presley in Heaven
By Hans Ostrom

They call each other *E*. Elvis picks
wildflowers near the river and brings
them to Emily. She explains half-rhymes to him.

In heaven Emily wears her hair long, sports
Levis and western blouses with rhinestones.
Elvis is lean again, wears baggy trousers

and T-shirts, a letterman's jacket from Tupelo High.
They take long walks and often hold hands.
She prefers they remain just friends. Forever.

Emily's poems now contain naugahyde, Cadillacs,
Electricity, jets, TV, Little Richard and Richard
Nixon. The rock-a-billy rhythm makes her smile.

Elvis likes himself with style. This afternoon
He will play the guitar and sing "I Taste a Liquor
Never Brewed" to the tune of "Love Me Tender."

Emily will clap and harmonize. Alone
in their cabins later, they'll listen to the river
And nap. They will not think of Amherst

or Las Vegas. They know why God made them
roommates. It's because America
was their hometown. It's because

God is a thing without
feathers. It's because
God wears blue suede shoes.

Window Shopping

Now you are ready to start looking for some inspirational clothes that help 'embody' and make visible who you are—according to your *own* self-definition. Set your mind on 'window shopping' mode, a fun time of wandering and browsing; considering this or perhaps that, with no pressure to buy—unless you just can't help yourself! Syd and Jasey began their quest with a catalogue; if you can't physically get out to the shops, start there. Storybook illustrations, greeting cards and other works of art also inspire me. Do a little internet surfing or wander around town and look at interesting people to get some ideas. Remember that Brenda and Sara saw their glad rags in their 'mind's eye' first and proceeded from there.

Things to Keep in Mind

Whatever your point of inspiration, as you set out to create your glad rag experience, here are some fun points to keep in mind:

1. Be creative

Realize that YOU are a work of art in process. Feel free to create and re-create yourself through the clothes you pull on, step into, and wrap around yourself. If it doesn't fit, take it off, take it in, alter it altogether until it suits you. Embellish it, up-cycle it or make it yourself. If you need to make it and can't sew, find someone to teach you—a friend, a neighbor, the fabric or craft store, the county extension agent or You Tube. You Tube has videos of just about everything you ever need to know. And don't forget, older neighbors often know how to do those very things that you would like to learn—like knit, embroider, quilt or sew.

2. Be playful

The most important thing you must do in your quest for glad rags is allow your sense of play and re-creation free rein. The most important thing to lead with, therefore, is a sense of *playfulness*. Embark on your journey by checking your inner critic at the door. You don't need that voice in your head nagging your socks down and spoiling your fun before you even get started. Bring your child-self to the forefront and see the potential in everything and anything. Remember Tammy, 'fussy-cutting' garments, finding a row of buttons or a pocket that she fancies and putting them in a pile for later use. You can do that too.

3. Shop smart

Make it easy to say yes. An easy way to silence the chattering of your inner critic is to indulge in Goodwill hunting, yard sale cruising, consignment and thrift store shopping as well as eBay, Craig's list, *Etsy* and other such sites. Not only are you more likely to encounter the quirky, the eccentric and the unique, you also may pay relatively little for it. Plus your purchase often supports a good cause or an independent business or artist, an entirely win-win situation.

4. Find ways to wear it

It doesn't have to 'make sense' or be practical. You don't have to have someplace specific to wear it. If you love the thing, buy it (or make it) and take it home. Even if you only ever wear it in your own house or your own back yard, it is important to have it where you can look at it, touch it, put it on. Invite yourself to a midnight meal with wine and favorite food and wear your beautiful dress. Light a candle and toast yourself. Create an event—like Tina and her friends did with their 'inappropriate cocktail parties.' Your glad rags feed your soul and no one else can tell you what you should or shouldn't wear to the banquet.

5. Feel it

Whatever challenge or problem you are struggling with or quest you are considering undertaking, hold it loosely in your mind and then simply open yourself to inspiration. Don't get hung up on 'solving' the problem or finding a concrete answer because you may not even be asking the right questions. Simply be aware of things you encounter that get your attention and move you in some way. If you burst out laughing, like Barbara did when she found her Buffalo hide boots, you are probably on the right track. If the feel, the shape or outrageousness of something delights you, like Amy's Super Girl underpants, you have probably found it. Be awake, pay attention—life is not a dress rehearsal.

Shop 'Til You Smile!

As we have seen, anything you can put on your body qualifies as glad rags. Glad rags are your best clothes—clothes that make you happy, make you feel attractive, comforted, empowered, silly or just more alive!

To prime my creativity pump, I like to think of categories of clothes metaphorically, as standing for *something* I am looking to bring into my life. It helps put me in a more playful mood as I cruise yard sales or flea markets if I am thinking in terms of finding a coat for slaying dragons, or boots for dancing on Mars, or buttons or bows to adorn a hat to wear to tea with the Queen. It puts me in a much more positive state of mind than if I am thinking, as many people do: "<sigh> Don't know why I bother even stopping. I never find anything good at these things <sigh>."

This is, of course, an active exercise in exaggeration. That 'dragon' could well be your boss or your ex or a pushy fitness coach. What else is playtime all about? All bets are off and this is your fantasy; you have permission to run with it. Playing is the place to start, to see where it might take you. Then you can consider what kind of inspiring clothes you might need along the way.

Let's just check the virtual *Marvelous Magical Mall* directory, shall we? Let's just see what goodies we can find to play with.

Boots and Shoes

From what I have observed, the two categories of footwear that most inspire women are boots, like Sophia's red cowgirl boots, and high heel shoes, like Helen's Guccis. High heel shoes are a cultural

marker, signifying that a girl has become a woman. They represent the freedom of adulthood and are specifically associated with sexuality. Color is of high importance as well. Inspiring footwear is very often red, which makes sense since we associate red with both passion and courage; although other colors, like blue suede shoes, might strike a responsive chord as well.

Boots and shoes are all about setting out on a journey and moving through time and space. You might consider what heights you want to attain: climbing to the mountaintop or scrambling up and over that chain link fence? Perhaps you would rather descend soundlessly into canyons, moving like a shadow across the canyon floor. Who are your companions? A wild and rowdy bunch of cowboys or pirates, the queen's own attendants, or perhaps none, other than an animal familiar? Let the questions float freely and be prepared to take an entirely unexpected direction based on what you might encounter.

I have a number of different pairs of boots in my glad rags stable and many others that have come and go. In the middle of writing this book I even stumbled across a pair of red cowgirl boots with fancy stitching in a consignment store that were just my size. Kismet! I was thrilled. But after a week or so, it was clear we were not compatible. We just didn't click.

"Why?" I asked them. "What is it that's not working?"

They shuffled and scuffed for a few moments and then I knew. I'm not a cowgirl. I was born in England; I'm not from here. I was disappointed but knew they were right, and so I gave them away to my native-born daughter and it was love at first sight. I wished them well and walked away.

A month later I came across a pair of plain, unadorned boots. I passed them by the first time, but they were a deep aqua and they beckoned me, so I came back.

"Really?" I said skeptically. "You're not even cowgirl boots."

"You're not a cowgirl," they countered…and I had to agree.

"Why would I buy you?" I asked. "Where would I wear you?"

"Because we are the color of mermaids," they said, "and we will take you dancing in the rain."

And so I bought them and shortly thereafter wore them, when my band played on the street for a farmer's market. It poured down rain and all the people danced anyway.

Hats and Headdresses

Things we wear on our head traditionally indicate status, role and office. Royalty wear crowns and you can

be sure that the queen's crown is always bigger than the princess's crown, a fact that Tina is well aware of! In the academic community, during convocations and other ceremonies on campus, a Ph.D. wears a lovely velvet Tudor bonnet, whereas undergraduates wear stiff, square mortarboards with tassels. A military officer wears a peaked cap and enlisted men and women wear fatigue or Garrison caps. No one has any doubt about who outranks whom and who is the top dog in any of these situations. Status is clearly indicated by who is allowed to wear what upon their heads.

In our busy society, particularly in the case of women, we often use the phrase 'juggling many hats' to refer to many of the different roles we play—such as mother, wife, bookkeeper, hostess, athletic coach, entrepreneur, spiritual advisor, nurse, dog walker, and so on. One person, many roles—hence, 'many hats.' In considering her hat choices, Renna poses the question, "Who am I today?" because, depending on the day, or the hour or the occasion, the answer might be different!

When I am considering hats, I start looking for a 'becoming' hat. It used to be a common descriptor of clothing, although the term is not often used now. It meant, 'attractive' and 'well-suited.' I like to consider the double meaning—that of 'attractive' as well as 'in process.' I open my mind to the notion of "What would I like to become?" The response *can* be purely pragmatic, as in, "I'd like to become warm!" in which case that fur lined watch cap might be just the thing! Alternatively, the response might be, "I'd like to become someone who rides off into the sunset," and then perhaps I will find just the right cowgirl hat or a warrior queen's helmet.

Hats are fertile ground for 'hands on' experimentation. With the help of a trusty glue gun or needle and thread, anyone can embellish and update a hat. You can wear several hats at a time, piling up two or three gossamer garden party hats and then tying them down with a saucy silk scarf, or a paisley head wrap tucked under a white Panama hat. You can also experiment with tiaras and flower and beribboned headbands, as well as feathered clips, fascinators and deelie boppers. Suzelle's phrase of hats being 'a party on your head' often guides my search as well.

What would you like to become? It is entirely up to you; play around, make it up, have fun. A great advantage of hats is that you can whisk them on or off in a second. I always think of hats as mini-costumes in that they don't require a long-term commitment. If, after an hour or two of being the belle of the ball in your party hat, you wish to be an anonymous face in the crowd at the grocery store, all you have to do is take off the hat and leave it in the car.

And one is cautioned not to engage in a love affair with a hat: it happens more than most people like to admit. For example, one weekend I wore my hand-made, felted burnt orange elf hat with the deep green curlicue on top to the grocery store. I rang the bell on the deli counter and the tattooed young woman slicing corned beef turned around and gasped in awe. "No f*%king way!" she breathed. "Are you fairy folk? Are you one of the *fae*? Do you know Starr Willow who lives near Ashley? You can find her on Facebook –she has a website. You gotta meet her! Oh my God!"

I hardly knew what to say. I believe if the deli counter had not been so tall she would have vaulted over and kissed my hand. I smiled vaguely and nodded and moved on, clutching my sliced, center-cut Swiss cheese in front of me like a gentle shield.

A week later, I returned to the deli counter, wearing one of my more modest, deep purple fleece hats with a matching bow. The young woman was there again but

this time did not signify at all. She called me "ma'am,"
sliced my cheese and handed me the package without
even a trace of recognition. I am sure it was a classic
case of the *Love Hat Relationship.*

The Love-Hat Relationship
By Aaron Belz (for Morgan Lael)

I have been thinking about the love-hat relationship.
It is the relationship based on love of one another's hats.
The problem with the love-hat relationship is that it is superficial.
You don't necessarily even know the other person.
Also it is too dependent on whether the other person
is even wearing the favored hat. We all enjoy hats,
but they're not something to build an entire relationship on.
My advice to young people is to like hats but not love them.
Try having like-hat relationships with one another.
See if you can find something interesting about
the personality of the person whose hat you like.

Socks, Stockings and Undies

Socks and underwear are 'kissing cousins' in that they can be worn in such a manner that no one else sees them. I love the idea of wearing outrageous polka dot socks under an entirely proper black pants suit, or a pair of monkey socks beneath a conservative skirt and boots. You can wear a lacy thong or tiger-striped bra under your postal uniform and no one's the wiser. It's a bit like having a giggle up your pants or a snicker under your skirt. When you work in a job that requires a certain dress code or uniform, wearing fun underwear or interesting socks helps maintain a sense of individuality—just as Rae's colorful Dream Hats did in the Operating Room. On your home turf, you can also opt to wear socks as proudly and loudly as you desire.

As much as I delight in my stash of flashy socks, at the end of the day, I always come home to my comfy, hand-knitted socks. Keeping in mind that while glad rags can be fun, they are also clothes you feel relaxed in, at home in—comfort clothes. I live in a part of the country that is often besieged with snow and windy weather, so I find that socks are right up there as some of my favorite comfort clothes. What better feeling than to come home from a hard day at the office, peel off those stockings, kick off the heels and sink your tootsies deep into their soft, warm embrace. Yummy!

Cris, my clever daughter-in-law, knitted me a pair of long, sturdy socks for Christmas a few years ago, and they have been a blessing. My office was built as an addition to our house, so it has three outside walls and a chilly floor without benefit of an insulating basement. These socks are my glad rags, my 'sole mates,' for sure. They keep my feet warm and snuggle up around my calves as well. I don't know what I'd do without them!

Stockings, like high heels, have always been a cultural marker of womanhood. I recall my mother telling me that during WWII when young women were unable to get nylon stockings, they drew the seam on their legs with a black eyebrow pencil in order to look 'proper.'

Back in the day when women in the workplace were not permitted to wear pants—even within my memory—stockings were a required part of the 'professional' dress code. Putting on and taking off stockings became one of those transitional experiences: you knew you were home and 'free' when you took your stockings off.

Then along came the swinging 60s and stockings got to be all kinds of fun. Stockings were no longer basic black, navy, beige, white or gray; they were suddenly patterned and colored in all manner of intriguing designs. Wrapped in tissue paper in my sock drawer is a pair of my most treasured glad rags ever: seriously silver stockings purchased in Chelsea, a section of London frequented by the Beatles and other hip young rockers. I still take those stockings out occasionally just to soak up their magical presence.

In all the playing and fun associated with glad rags, however, it is important to note that some rules are inviolable. Both in the case of underwear and socks—bottom line—they have to fit and be comfortable. Most women will adapt to shoe and boot sizes if the awesomeness of the footwear warrants it; we tell ourselves that we will wear an extra pair of socks to make them fit or just wear them to make an entrance to the party then *sit down* for the rest of the evening—but you can't fake it with socks or underwear. They have to fit.

The questions I ask as I underwear and sock shop tend to be more sober:

"Can I see myself in a long term relationship with you?"

"Will you be there for me and stay up with me, without my having to ask?"

"Can you keep up when I have to run flat out?"

"Will you keep my most intimate secrets secret?"

"Do you promise to never embarrass me by falling down unexpectedly in the middle of a business seminar?"

If I sense any hesitation at all, I move on. Some things just aren't negotiable.

Jeans - Glad Rags for a Generation & Beyond

As I was chatting with Syd, she happened to mention how important being able to wear blue jeans had been in her life, that blue jeans were definitely her glad rags. "For me, blue jeans are a symbol of freedom," she said. She fought the good fight to end dress codes for women on campus in the 70s and found it ironic that as a teacher, she was not allowed to wear jeans on the job. She is happy to have retired from teaching so she can wear jeans whenever she feels so inclined.

The more I thought about it, the more it seemed to me that blue jeans are a category unto themselves—cultural glad rags for Americans in general. Blue jeans started out as hard-wearing pants for hard working people, first manufactured by Levi Strauss, a German-Jewish immigrant in the late 1800s. By the 1920s they were the established uniform of miners, cowboys, lumberjacks and railroad men—men who made a living by the sweat of their brows and the strength of their backs.

Jeans began their climb to universal fame in the late 1950s, riding the backside of a rising, rebellious youth culture heralded by the scandalous beat of rock and roll. Bill Haley and his Comets released *Rock Around the Clock* in 1954, the song that Wikipedia describes as "the anthem of youth culture that brought rock and roll into the mainstream around the world." Haley urged his ladies to "put your glad rags on and join me, hon; we'll have fun till the clock strikes one…"

Parents like mine warned daughters not to date the sort of boy who would wear jeans on a date. During the musical 'British Invasion' of the 60s, the Beatles came over charming, well-groomed and wearing tailored trousers; the Rolling Stones, ruffians in tight jeans, looked like they had just come from a pub fight.

Dress codes relaxed in the middle to late 60s and women finally were permitted to wear pants to the office as well as to school. It was 'bye-bye!' to frozen gams at the bus stop and an end to having Mr. Price peer up your skirt when you were on the library ladder re-shelving books. The line was drawn, however, when it came to blue jeans. They were still too 'casual' and often considered 'disreputable,' making them highly desirable to headstrong teens.

Jeans, the unassuming pants of the working class, became a political icon during the social upheaval and

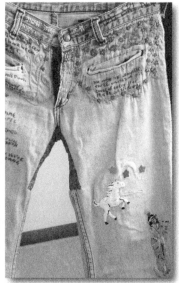

counterculture revolution of the later 60s. During the 'summer of love,' jeans relaxed under the influence of flower power as they also became the 'peace out' uniform of choice for hippies. Soon those jeans were covered with embroidery, buttons and all kinds of colorful embellishment. Because the Boomer generation came of age while wearing blue jeans, and because that era was so intensely political, jeans themselves were saturated with political significance.

Boomers grew up, entered business, became community leaders, bought houses in the suburbs and raised families. In true 'melting pot' American fashion, what was once a dynamic subgroup became mainstream by process of assimilation. In similar manner, jeans became re-designed, re-branded and reputable, and eventually became available in every style and size imaginable.

Almost everyone has a favorite pair of blue jeans and a fond leisure time memory to go with them. Blue jeans are so democratic, suitable for all Americans; blue jeans just feel like 'home.'

So as I apply glad rags consideration while jeans shopping, I consider my own personal politics. But am I looking for love and understanding in all the wrong places? Maybe I am a fickle *Venus in Blue Jeans* or perhaps a saucy *Mustang Sally* with my hair in braids? Will I wear my faded blue jeans to a gritty work camp in Appalachia or purchase designer jeans to pair with stiletto heels to an indie film screening? Can I be all of those women and play with all of those roles? If I am only allowed one pair of pants for my next life, blue jeans, could it be you?

Add-ons and Accessories

Accessories are like grace notes in the world of glad rags, a little something extra to sweeten the pot. During my mother's generation, the wearing of accessories was governed by strict rules, which also applied to the rest of a woman's wardrobe. Pocketbooks, for instance, were to match shoe color as closely as possible and if not, should repeat a prominent color in the outfit. White shoes and handbags were *only* permitted between Memorial Day and Labor Day. It was the law of the land, enforced by the fashion police nationwide. Bare legs, even with sandals, were a no-no, except at the beach.

Pocketbooks

Once again, during the 60s when rules of conduct shook themselves free of previous constraints, rules of dress followed suit. Pocketbooks were released from the tyranny of 'The Outfit' where everything matched. Proper little handbags were optional and color was entirely up to the wearer. Free spirited adventurers set the tone with backpacks and ethnic bags of many stripes, which they stuffed full of both essential and frivolous gear.

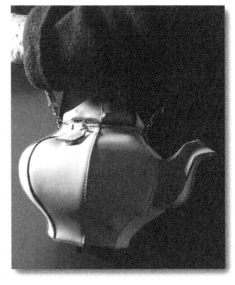

For some women, a pocketbook is an essential and carefully guarded stronghold. Touch their pocketbook and they will bite your hand off.

"I am really particular about my pocketbook," says Oshun, shifting her pocketbook closer. "It carries all my important stuff."

These ladies do not feel 'dressed' or secure without a pocketbook and wouldn't consider leaving home without it. For them, a pocketbook often contains essential supplies like makeup, wallet, phone and keys, as well as a unique collection of personal artifacts, like socks, snacks and breath mints; phone charger, wipes, tissues, an extra diaper, crayons, small towel and dog treats; last month's utility bill, take out menu, hair dryer and rain hat. Others, like Cris, see pocketbooks as entirely optional—a hindrance and a bother—and they are likely to stuff their keys and change in a coat pocket and slip out unencumbered.

For Riley, pocketbooks are jewels, her pets and treasures. A connoisseur, she searches out rare and vibrant colors, whimsical shapes and sizes to add to her vast collection. Amanda, on the other hand, collects a specific name brand and prizes them all like trophies.

Bottom line, pocketbooks are like unpredictable children—separate from you, but obviously connected to you in an intimate way. They can reflect well or badly on you and this can change without warning. They can work on your behalf or frustrate you at every turn. They can wriggle from your grasp, throw themselves recklessly to ground, making public the most intimate secrets of your life for all the world to see. Some pocketbooks present a smooth and blank face to the world, while inside they seethe with clutter and chaos. Others are a study in whimsy and misdirection on the outside but silent and mysterious on the inside.

Remember what your mother said about always wearing clean underwear in case you were in an accident and had to go to the hospital? Your pocketbook is like that. As I am evaluating a pocketbook for a possible glad rags experience, I ask myself, "If I were in an accident or got abducted by aliens and someone had to extrapolate my life and personality based on this particular pocketbook, what kind of person might they imagine me to be—and how would I feel about that?" I eye the pocketbook warily, pick it up, throw it up on my shoulder, tuck it under my arm. *Can I trust it*? I wonder.

"Will you behave and keep all my important stuff neat and organized and promise not to throw everything to the bottom where I can't find it, or hide my lip gloss in your lining when I'm not looking?"

Although pocketbooks require a firm hand, I confess to being easily led astray by a seductive shape, color or abundance of zippered compartments. In a classic example, during a visit to Covent Garden in London a few years ago, I spied a blue leather pocketbook shaped like an English teapot in the window of a small boutique. I squealed with delight, threw caution to the winds, ran in and purchased it on the spot. It was a pocketbook that would not be denied; hence, an example of the authentic glad rags experience.

Glasses

Although glasses have always had a specific function—to improve vision or to protect eyes from glare—at the same time, there they are, smack dab on the middle of your face. Glasses can be unobtrusive

or outrageous and still leave an indelible impression of who you are to anyone who sees you. It is hard to think of the legendary rock icon Buddy Holly, for instance, without immediately picturing his black-framed glasses. In my mind's eve, John Lennon is always wearing wire rimmed granny glasses, although for much of his performing career he wore no glasses at all. Jackie-O made sunglasses glamorous in a way no one else ever did, and Elton John took eyeglass fashion to a whole new level!

Tammy colors a generous portion of her hair a rich purple and has chosen purple eyeglass frames to match. No one is ever going to forget her colorful face! Cris buys inexpensive, gel-colored glasses online by the handful and wears whichever pair matches her mood or outfit that day. Horn or wire rimmed glasses want you to take them seriously—or, alternatively, they help the wearer maintain a low profile.

Glasses technically fall into a *function* rather than *form* category, but with all the options available and the many ways women wear them, eyeglasses are worthy candidates for the glad rags experience.

There are so many other accessories to play with, like gloves and arm warmers, scarves, cowls, belts, hair wraps and gee jaws—all up for your consideration as you window shop in the glad rags bazaar. Try them all on, dance in them, fly with them and find some more.

You've done some window shopping, had some fun. Now is time to sort through your treasure trove of impressions and sensations, golden shoes and tweedy vests, to discover which pieces truly inspired and delighted you and go get them, one way or another. You are your own work in process, your own work of art, and you deserve all your best creative input and joyful output. I hope you have enjoyed the shopping trip. Stop by the wrap up desk in the next chapter on your way out. Let's do this again soon!

Threads

Sweet and Sentimental

I remembered that Mother had a pair of lace gloves that were always in her top drawer, wrapped in tissue paper. They were quite fancy—a gift that my father had given her that he brought back from Paris. They weren't her style, but she saved them all of her life because it was the first gift he gave her after they were married.

My parents met during WWII. It was England in the 1940s. They were both in the service—my father in the Royal Navy and mother in the Army—and they both loved to dance. They met in a ballroom, discovered that they were natural partners, and danced the night away. Four or five weeks later they married, and two days after that, my father was shipped overseas for the Invasion.

Mother didn't see him again for more than a year, after the war was finally over. When he came home he brought her the gloves, wrapped in tissue paper. They were beautiful and exotic and I don't think she ever wore them. She had a thing about not wearing dark or 'drab' clothing—perhaps because of her grueling childhood and experiences during the war—and the gloves were midnight blue, very nearly black.

When she died and I was clearing out her closet, there was not one single item of clothing that was

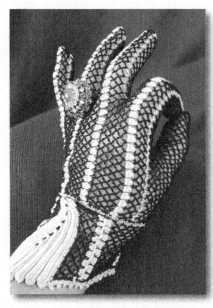

black, olive drab or dark gray. She avoided them on principal. She wore Hawaiian shirts and Mexican dresses, floral blouses and jewel-toned skirts. Even her socks had butterflies and rainbows embroidered on them.

But as I was writing this book, I remembered those gloves and began searching through the drawer where I keep the few bits and pieces she left behind. I found them finally, tucked inside an evening bag, and I had to slip them on. It immediately called up an image of my parents, who loved nothing better than to put on their glad rags and go out dancing—something they did right up until my father died suddenly, in his mid-50s.

Mother, an accomplished seamstress, would wear one of the several dresses that she had made herself—a peacock blue brocade, orange sherbert organza, and emerald green silk, all embellished with ribbon or lace trim. She wore strappy, high-heeled sandals and a soft wrap, shot through with silver thread.

I can still hear their music playing in my head, like "In the Mood" and all the fat sounds of the Big Bands like the Dorsey Brothers and Artie Shaw. I see my father, in his suit and polished shoes, standing and extending his hand to her and then, in my mind's eye, I see them gliding across the dance floor through eternity, smiling for all they are worth.

Dressing Up...Everybody Gets to Play

When I first met Liz she played banjo in a 'back porch' band. Most of the folks played for fun, but mixed in were a few outstanding musicians. Mike was one of them. Not only could he play the fiddle like nobody's business; he had that kind of mind that could pick up and play a tune in about two seconds, no matter whether you sang it or played a snatch or showed him a few bars you had written out on a scrap of paper. He was a really nice guy and a totally awesome musician. When Liz and Mike got married, soon after that she put aside her banjo and stopped playing altogether.

"Mike is such an incredible fiddle player," she said. "He can play anything. I had to work really hard at my banjo playing and I simply could not keep up. So I stopped frustrating myself and just stopped playing."

Have you ever been to a concert, watched a performance or viewed a piece of art created by someone who is a virtuoso, a genius? If it is in a field that you greatly admire or a skill that you dream about learning, you may find it so overwhelming, so awesome, that instead of feeling inspired, you feel depressed. Sometimes such encounter makes you feel diminished, ashamed even. In the face of such talent, skill, art, grace, whatever—you feel like giving up that precious thing that you cherish in your heart: playing the piano, soccer, drawing, dancing, baking, writing— anything. You want to throw your saxophone into the creek, rip up your drawing, give your dancing shoes to the first passerby.

"Who am I? What was I thinking?" we say. "I shouldn't even try."

How many of us have been in that position? (Trust me, my hand is in the air as well…)

When I was young, I totally loved the theatre and performing in just about every guise: dance, music, drama, I loved it all—the costumes, lights, music. I loved the idea of creating a world apart from the mundane, everyday life that, for me, was sometimes just *too* ordinary.

Alas, the moment I stepped onto the stage, I froze. I was very good at disappearing, escaping notice, being quiet—skills that did not serve me well on the stage. I studied drama in high school and college, took guitar and dance lessons—but I was pretty much a wash out when it actually came to performing. I was better as a stage manager and only in my dreams was I any good in front of the curtain.

Then the year I turned 30, when my life was turned upside down, I learned how to juggle and became a street performer. I went on the road on an open-ended bicycle trip and juggled on street corners all over New England. There were no auditions, no lines to memorize, no sets and lighting cues; no admission, no charge and no pressure. We made it up on the fly. It was fun and silly and everyone had a good time. If it just wasn't happening on that day at that time, we packed up our hat and clubs, hopped back on our bicycles and pedaled on down the road.

My partner was a much more experienced and skilled juggler than I was. He talked a mile a minute, and he could juggle more balls and objects than I ever could; but it didn't matter. We created routines in which he was the swaggering 'star' and I was the silent assistant. Then, unexpectedly, I would walk into the scene and steal the balls or the hat. We played it for high hilarity and the audience loved it. And, inevitably, I was the one the children approached. I remember one little girl in particular, who was standing beside me as my partner was doing a flashy solo piece. "I wish I could do that," she said wistfully, watching the brightly colored balls dance in the air.

"You can," I said. "Let me show you how." And I taught her on the spot how to juggle three balls.

Did I go on to be a great performer? Did I go on tour and get booked into Vegas? No. We went on tour, but it was on bicycles, and the people we played for were businessmen on lunch break, waitresses, students on the way to class, grandparents out for a stroll—and kids, lots of kids. We had a wonderful time and invited a lot of people to come out to play with us.

People don't stop to watch street performers because they have to—they have not paid for tickets, it wasn't on their calendar and they are, in fact, usually rushing to SOMEPLACE ELSE. They stop to watch street performers because they simply cannot help themselves; they are ambushed by delight.

We also discovered that one of the reasons people liked us was *because* we weren't virtuosos; we were kind of like the people in the audience; they could identify with us. We dropped props and made dumb jokes. We included smart aleck kids and crotchety old men in our shows. When people watched us, their response was more apt to be: "Maybe I *could* do that"—or, at the very least, they appreciated someone out there having fun and doing something interesting, even if every throw wasn't perfect. Folks were *encouraged*, not discouraged, from giving it a try—whatever 'it' happened to be in their lives. There were people we met who, inspired by what they experienced, went home and started making their own kind of music, apple pies or hats or puppet shows or whatever.

In my world, it was just about the best thing I had ever done—have ever done. I helped people feel happy and empowered, added something to the 'plus' side of the life equation.

I also discovered along the way—as I went on to do arts outreach, working with 'populations at risk'—that when I handed someone an interesting hat and they put it on, the effect was often instantaneous and transformational. They saw themselves in a whole different light—and more importantly, they had been given permission to play. When I wear one of my somewhat eccentric, fun hats out in the community now, many people react enthusiastically to my hats as well. They want to play, too.

The same dynamic that I discovered in street performing applies to glad rags as well. People can't help but respond; they are ambushed by delight.

Clothes are available to all of us; they require no special skill, knowledge, technology or art supplies. You don't have to write about it or create a drawing or collage—although, of course, you *can* do that if

you are so inclined. You simply put them on. You can try them on, take them off and try on something else. What could be more natural? In my subsequent work, I began collecting not only hats but also stories about the transformational power of clothes in (mostly) women's lives.

The stories in this book are like that. There is no blueprint for success here, no 'Five Steps to a Richer and Sexier You.' There are simply true stories of real women who stepped onto the stage—in spite of all the odds, in spite of all their fears and self-doubts—and became heroines in their own stories. Sometimes it required that they change the story and adapt the role they had been assigned to play—and they did that too.

Every one of you has a story to tell and a song to sing. Every one of you has a dream and it is very possible you may be selling yourself short, thinking it is an 'impossible dream.' But perhaps if you start with an outrageous pair of underpants or some kicking red boots, you will find a bit of courage to take the next step—and then the next one and the next one after that. The sky is the limit.

So I encourage you, invite you, to put on your glad rags, pull up your sassy-ass sassafras underpants, lace up your traveling shoes. Have some fun, change your luck, change the world.

Postscript

Join Me Online to Keep the Glad Rags Experience Going!

The one intriguing thing that so many women said during the interviews was that their glad rags experience often prompted the sharing of stories. Tammy says that everyone seems to have a 'Red Panty' story they are eager to share with her; Tina says that people who buy her tiaras tell her about all the different ways the tiaras have made their lives more fun. I mentioned how often glad rags are shared with friends and family—Judy's 'da Coat, Sophia's red cowgirl boots. I can attest to the number of times I have worn one of my hats out in public and someone will come up and share stories with me about a hat their mother wore, or one that they had owned and always loved—or they simply ask to take my photo (to take a photo of my hat, to be more precise!). In any case, and in every instance, the article of clothing—

glad rags—gives other people an opening, the means by which they can engage in face-to-face conversation.

One of my primary motivations in writing this book was to create a fun and inclusive environment for women to share their stories—which is why I so entirely enjoyed writing this book. I had such a great time with this project that frankly, I don't want it to end. I want to hear and see more from all of you. I will have a dedicated web page and blog for the book and would really love it, if you feel so moved, to share your stories and photos. I have only scratched the surface and would love to keep the conversation going.

Visit www.GladRagsProject.com

Appendix A

Shop in the Marketplace

In Part II of this book I introduce some remarkable women who have taken their own glad rags experience and run with it, creating more garments for the delight or comfort of others. If you were intrigued by or attracted to the glad rags these women have created and offer for sale, here's how you can find out more online:

Brenda Jones—Hug Wraps www.hugwraps.org (Facebook page—Hug Wraps)

Rae Ream, RN, BSN, CNOR—Dream Hats www.dreamhats.org (Facebook page—Dream Hats, Inc.)

Tina Kelsey - Tina's Tiaras www.tinastiaras.com

Tammy Perakis Wallace—Red Panty Designs www.etsy.com/shop/RedPantyDesigns

Amy Robbin Becraft (Super Girl underpants)—
Mary Kay regional manager www.marykay.com to
find a consultant in your area

Rev. Suzelle Lynch (Hat Theology) www.uucw.org
(uurevlynch@gmail.com)

Helen Owens (in her shoes) - Her Secret Hair
Extensions www.hersecrethairextensions.com

Linda Severance Bennet (Facebook page—
WhimseyWear)

Appendix B

Kickstarter Project Donors

With a Little Help from My Friends…and Kickstarter

A great big thank you and shout out to all the lovely people who contributed to my Kickstarter project that helped get this book launched; in no particular order:

Peg Watkins
Marge Diamond
Angela Miller
Garbo Seltzer
Linda Severance Bennett
Doug Berch
Penny Parsons
Vicki Lefevre
Andrea Chmelik
Oshun Allen
Naomi Kayne
Marilyn Mars

David Soliday
Nancy Smeltzer
Amy Bennett
Elizabeth Garrabrant
Sydney Schnaars
Donna Wellman Russell
Judith Johnson
Elizabeth Harzoff
Kate Rander Pinto
Ralph Leesberg
Colleen Huckabee
Tammy Wallace
Diana de la Mer
Iris Allen
Liz Greene
Noelle Byrum
Maureen Day
Carl Yaffey
Tina Carnes Kelsey
Anna Travis
Karen Poremski
Margaret Day
Steve Pinsky